ART OF THE STATE
STATE OF THE ART

ART OF THE STATE

Massachusetts Photographers, 1975-1977

Edited by S U S A N R. C H A N N I N G
with an Introduction by E S T E L L E J U S S I M

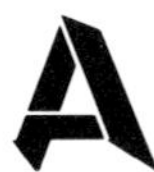

Published by the Massachusetts Arts and Humanities Foundation, Inc.
in association with Addison House, Danbury, New Hampshire

ISBN 0-891-69-034-4
LC 78-51086

For permission to reproduce any of these photographs, or for
information about purchasing, renting, exhibiting or other-
wise using the work, please write to the Massachusetts Arts
and Humanities Foundation, 100 Boylston Street, Boston,
Massachusetts 02116.

Publication of this book was made possible, in part, by grants
from the Polaroid Foundation, Inc., and the National Endowment for the Arts in Washington, D. C., a Federal agency.

Designed by Katy Homans
Printed by Thomas Todd Co., Boston
Introduction by Estelle Jussim © 1978 Estelle Jussim

Introduction
Looking at Winners

Photography is in its hey-day. It has reached the apex of its popularity, its influence, its critical acclaim. It is chic. It is fashionable. It is produced, exhibited, purchased and pursued with the same modish flamboyance which once erupted over abstract expressionism and pop art. It is perhaps the only visual art which demonstrates such vigor, such exuberance, such accessibility. Schools of photographic practice, university programs in the history of photography, journals devoted to photographic criticism, books about, by, and for photographers proliferate in all languages, all countries, on all levels of quality. The local amateurs' clubs are more active than ever.

It is not surprising, therefore, that foundations have undertaken the responsibility to support the serious artist of photography with increasing numbers of fellowships and grants. It is even less surprising that the Commonwealth of Massachusetts — a state with a distinguished history of photographic enterprise and creativity from Southworth and Hawes to Minor White — should be expanding its activities as a great center for all things photographic. And it is agreeable in the extreme that a mere three years of competition for fellowships from the Massachusetts Arts and Humanities Foundation should have produced such a splendid selection of prints as are here reproduced.

Having remarked these facts, there nevertheless remain some problems which we should confront before examining the images themselves. We know that over one thousand portfolios were examined, each containing the photographer's choice of his or her own "best ten" prints. Yet the question immediately arises in the evaluation of any gleaning from foundation competitions: is this collection of winners to be regarded as an idiosyncratic outcome, more representative of the pet ideologies of well-known panelists — themselves photographers — than of some state of the art of photography in the larger sense? What will we learn from this collection? Will the prints reveal some geographic bias, some regionally incestuous obsession which might mark the closely-knit community of photographers in Massachusetts? Or will we discover tendencies which universally brand the decade of the 1970's? Will the images speak meekly of academic assignments, or bravely of individual inventiveness? Will it prove to be *enough* that these photographers were selected as the "best" out of that vast anonymous mass of portfolios and slides? Is it enough to have been thought "the best" at a particular moment in the history of a medium in a particular region? And finally, most importantly, what does it mean to be thought "the best"?

Any foundation panel inevitably encounters the almost unendurable truth that financial limitations must force the selection of the very few and the rejection of the very many. The choice must obviously grow out of compromise and the necessities of creating consensus. But, just as inevitably, this requires not only that many a mute, inglorious Milton may bloom unseen, but that photographers of notable achievements must be, will be, ignored. It is the same problem which probably irritated the jury of the Paris Exhibition of 1863, when, to its dismay and astonishment, Manet and a whole new school of art exploded in the Salon des Refusés. There may always be a culture lag between the invention of new forms in any art and the acceptance or recognition of those forms by even the most sophisticated judges.

Having bowed to these caveats, and acknowledging that there may be inequities in any foundation selection, we can turn with considerable pleasure to the images themselves. Here are pictures by photographers old and young, male and female, established and unknown, those frequently published and those whose work has never been published before. What we cannot see here are the subtleties of color originals, and, of course, even the black-and-white prints may have had to be considerably reduced to the format of this book. What we can see is a lively indication of the types of images presently capturing the imaginations of a wide range of artists. The nature of reproduction is such that it can only provide a map of a reality which must be encountered in its physical presence to be enjoyed. No matter how casually its reproductions are confused with its originals, photography demands an interaction with real artifacts. The experience of the purity of platinum prints is quite different from the etched velvet of photogravure. While books undoubtedly will continue to be the most efficient, economical and portable means of distribution for original images, no book can be a substitute gallery. In a very real sense, no book can be more than a beckoning to an encounter with the prints themselves.

The prints are as varied as the contemporary scene, and they clearly document the diversity of the 1970s' trends. Gone but not forgotten is the old documentary photograph which relied exclusively on the impact of the slice-of-life, where the camera revealed corners of reality with shock or with the irony and grand "accidents" of Weegee and Cartier-Bresson. A new conception of what constitutes a collision with reality emanates from the work of Jerome Liebling, where the outer realities are unflinchingly squeezed by a fierce individual perception which has the willingness to confront the painful fragilities of humanity, to press hard against the meaning of objects. The prints of Benno Friedman, on the other hand, represent a new photographic connection with the long tradition of the graphic arts, especially with the subtleties of drawing. The tension between the photographic foundation of the print and Friedman's graphic manipulations speaks of a reality which is a universal organizing structure.

Antitheses abound. The conceptual portraits of Wendy MacNeil, where the brooding multiples of tightly-knit images within images have the heady effect of mingling memory with desire, juggle time with poetic precision, while the zestful, risk-taking combinations by Ken Brown play with real/unreal, possible/impossible with the abandon of a surreal tiger. Kipton Kumler's decorative and often soaring architectural motifs collide with Bruce Kinch's complex three-dimensional landscapes which shimmer and gleam with an ominous formal rigor. Jonathan Morse's offset photo-lithographs, in their free-form collage combinations, are large originals with color, while Kevin Monaghan's smooth and subtle architectural landscapes, with their demarcated forms, are pure black-and-white endeavors, and quite small.

The turbulent, always controlled but almost overwhelming physical presence of the images of Chris Enos — the crescendo of water or the bursting, ravaging forms of cactus — ricochet off the quietness of Nancy Rankin, who makes a straightforward anthropology of adolescence. The profound and moving ambiguities of Carl Chiarenza's black textures, wherein the link to a reality which cannot be labeled disappears into an encounter with mystery, contrast in almost every conceivable way with the large color prints of Thomas Petit, whose use of free-form light and multiple images creates a mythological aura of uncertainty. And all the others offer their own special glimpses into the preoccupations of photographers today.

What is missing from this collection, we cannot say for sure; we all know that no photographer can be appreciated from a selection of only four prints. Nevertheless, it seems obvious that the doom-sayers who have recently begun to prophesy the imminent demise of photography have been entirely too pessimistic. Playing with time in a form once considered capable only of "stopping time," playing with ambiguities of photography versus calligraphy in a medium which long disdained any echo of pictorialist manipulation, playing with obscure surfaces and deceiving realities, these photographs are proof of the inordinate profusion of graphic media, combinations of images, and pure forms, which are available to artists today. They are striking demonstrations that the art of photography is alive and well in Massachusetts.

Estelle Jussim
Simmons College, Boston

Editor's Preface

Massachusetts has long been one of the nation's centers of photographic education, research and experimentation. The concentration of photographic resources and respected professionals has provided this region with an unusual range and depth of artistic development in photography. Thus, it is the intent of *Art of the State* . . . to provide photographers, photo-historians, and the public with an introduction to the . . . *State of the Art* in Massachusetts.

Art of the State . . . does not have a theme. Rather, it is an effort to assemble a permanent group exhibition of representative work by 18 outstanding Massachusetts photographers. These artists share one distinction that accounts for their inclusion here: they are all recipients of Artists Fellowships in photography awarded by the Massachusetts Arts and Humanities Foundation since 1975.

The Foundation, which is a private, non-profit organization, was incorporated in 1973 to provide direct and indirect financial and technical assistance to individual creative artists. To a significant degree, the Foundation's efforts complement the work of the state arts agency, the Massachusetts Council on the Arts and Humanities. While the Council works with arts and cultural organizations in the state, the Foundation amplifies the Council's efforts by working directly with the individual artists whose work constitutes the well-spring from which arts, cultural and other social institutions draw. The Council played the principal role in the conception and development of both the Foundation and its fellowship program and continues to provide substantial financial support to both.

The Artists Fellowship Program was the first and remains one of the principal Foundation programs. Since 1975, through the Artists Fellowship Program, the Foundation has awarded individual $3,000 fellowships to 160 poets, novelists and short-story writers, playwrights, filmmakers, video artists, composers, choreographers, painters, printmakers, sculptors, and photographers. These unrestricted fellowships are meant to affirm the work of outstanding Massachusetts artists and to assist them to continue their work in Massachusetts.

There is only one criterion for selection as a recipient in the Artists Fellowship Program: the quality of work the applicants submit for review. The panelists retained by the Foundation to review the artists' work are not given the applicants' names or any other biographical information. The panels for each of the 11 fields are composed of artists working in the field in which they serve. They are recommended by artists and administrators in and outside Massachusetts. They themselves must live outside the state. Panelists are different each year, and are chosen in an effort to reflect a wide range of critical artistic judgments and styles.

The 18 artists represented in this book received fellowships in 1975, 1976, and 1977. The first of each artist's four prints reproduced here was selected from the portfolio each artist submitted in the year he or she received a fellowship. The remaining three prints, some of which also are from the original portfolios, were selected in cooperation with the artists, in an effort to represent the range of the artist's work. While four prints cannot provide a comprehensive view of any individual, it is hoped that these will serve as useful introductions to the state of the art in Massachusetts. Finally, this collection provides the artists and the public with a permanent group exhibition that brings the work of these 18 fellowship recipients together for the first and, possibly, the only time.

I would like to express our gratitude to the artists represented here for their patient and enthusiastic help and to art historian and critic Estelle Jussim for contributing the Introduction to this book. The Foundation is especially indebted to the organizations whose financial support — of both the Foundation and the Artists Fellowship Program — has made publication of this book possible: The National Endowment for the Arts, a federal agency; the Massachusetts Council on the Arts and Humanities, the state arts agency; and the Polaroid Foundation, Inc.

Susan R. Channing, Director
Artists Fellowship Program

1975 Fellowship Recipients
Biographies

The panelists were BEN FERNANDEZ, LOTTE JACOBI, SYL LABROT, NATHAN LYONS and MARY ELLEN MARK. The five recipients were selected from 450 applicants.

CARL CHIARENZA, *Arlington*

Born 1935, Rochester, New York
Education: Rochester Institute of Technology, B.F.A.; Boston University, M.S., A.M.; Harvard University, Ph.D.

Carl Chiarenza has taught at Boston University since 1963 and is presently Associate Professor and Chairman, Department of Art History. He taught previously at the Visual Studies Workshop, Rochester, and is a consultant to the Polaroid Corporation. Chiarenza is the author of many articles and essays on photography and art history, and has given numerous lectures, workshops, seminars and symposia at photographic organizations and schools throughout the United States during the past 12 years.

Selected solo exhibitions

Carl Siembab Gallery, Boston, 1962, 1968, 1976, 1978 · Gallery 216, New York City, 1965 · Museum of Art, University of Oregon, Eugene, 1967 · Focus Gallery, San Francisco, 1968 · Phoenix College, Phoenix, Arizona, 1970 · The Cronin Gallery, Houston, Texas, 1976 · Western Carolina University, Cullowhee, North Carolina, 1977

Selected group exhibitions

(Chiarenza has been invited to participate in over 135 group exhibitions from 1957-1978)
Carl Siembab Gallery, Boston, annually, 1960-1978 · Museum of Modern Art, New York City, 1960 · Museum of Fine Arts, Boston, 1960 · DeYoung Museum, San Francisco, 1960 · Metropolitan Museum of Art, New York City, 1963 · George Eastman House, Rochester, New York, 1963 · Long Beach Museum of Art, Long Beach, California, 1964 · Yale University Art Gallery, New Haven, Connecticut, 1965 · Smithsonian Institution, Washington, D. C., 1967 · Minneapolis Institute of Arts, 1968 · U.C.L.A., 1968 · Fogg Art Museum, Cambridge, 1970 · University of Connecticut, Storrs, 1973 · Hayden Gallery, M.I.T., Cambridge, 1974 · International Center of Photography, New York City, 1975 · Art Institute of Chicago, 1975 · Worcester Art Museum, Massachusetts, 1977

Selected publications

Many articles on and reviews of photography, 1958-1977;

work reproduced in many catalogs, books and magazines. A few examples follow: *Modern Photography*, 1958; *Photography Yearbook*, London, 1962; *Aperture*, 1960, 1961, 1974; *The Encyclopedia of Photography*, 1963; *U. S. Camera*, 1964; *Photography*, London, 1965; *Contemporary Photographer*, 1964, 1965; *Photography in the Twentieth Century*, 1967; *Camera*, 1974.

Selected collections

International Museum of Photography, George Eastman House; U.C.L.A.; M.I.T.; Polaroid Corporation; Fogg Art Museum; Museum of Fine Arts, Houston; work in over 100 private collections.

Awards, prizes

Danforth Teacher Grants, 1966-1968; Kress Foundation Research Grant, 1970; National Endowment for the Arts Photography Fellowship 1977.

Mr. Chiarenza's black-and-white photographs appear on pp. 16 through 19.

CHRIS ENOS, *Boston*

Born 1944, California
Education: San Francisco State University, B.A.; San Francisco Art Institute, M.F.A.

Chris Enos is the founder and current Director of the Photographic Resource Center, Boston. She has taught photography at the San Francisco Academy of Art; Windham College, Putney, Vermont; Hampshire College, Amherst, Massachusetts; Boston University, Boston; Goddard College, Vermont; Harvard University, Cambridge; and New England School of Photography, Boston.

Selected solo exhibitions

M.I.T. Creative Photography Gallery, Cambridge, 1974 · Focus II Gallery, New York City, 1974 · Bibliothèque Nationale, Paris, 1975 · Carl Siembab Gallery, Boston, 1975 · Enjay Gallery, Boston, 1976 · University of California extension, San Francisco, 1976 · Camerawork Gallery, San Francisco, 1977 · University of Rochester, New York, 1977 · Pine Manor College, Chestnut Hill, Massachusetts, 1977

Selected group exhibitions

San Francisco Art Institute, 1969 · Hayden Gallery, M.I.T., 1971 · Baldwin Street Gallery, Toronto, 1972 · Light Gallery, New York City, 1974 · Fogg Art Museum, Cambridge, 1974 · Musée Française de la Photographie, Bièvres, France, 1976 · Museum of Fine Arts, Boston, 1976 · Vision Gallery, Boston, 1977 · Portland Museum, Maine, 1977

Selected collections

San Francisco Museum of Art; Bibliothèque Nationale, Paris; Fogg Art Museum; Museum of Fine Arts, Boston; Wellesley College, Massachusetts; private collections.

Selected publications

Aperture, 1971, 1972; *Camera 35*, 1973; *Viva, 1974;
Women's Photo Annual*, 1975; *Camera Magazine*, 1975;
Horticulture, 1975; *Women See Women*, 1976; *Boston
Globe*, 1977; *Images of Women*, 1977

Ms. Enos' black-and-white photographs appear on pp. 20
through 23.

B E N N O   F R I E D M A N , *Sheffield*

Born 1945, New York City
Education: Brandeis University, A.B.

Benno Friedman is a free-lance photographer. He has
taught or lectured at the Massachusetts College of Art,
Boston; San Francisco Art Institute; Wellesley College in
Massachusetts; Pratt School of Design, New York City;
Rhode Island School of Design, Providence; Apeiron
Workshops, Millertown, New York; International Center
for Photography, New York City; and M.I.T., Cambridge.
Using the camera-made negative, Friedman uses a range
of diverse materials and processes (solarization, toning,
bleaching, airbrushing, drawing, crayon and watercolor)
to make each color monoprint.

Selected solo exhibitions

Underground Gallery, New York City, 1969 · Addison
Gallery of American Art, Andover, Massachusetts, 1972 ·
Massachusetts College of Art, Boston, 1972 · Light Gallery,
New York City, 1973, 1975, 1976, 1977 · Tucson Art Cen-
ter, Arizona, 1973 · Columbia College, Chicago, 1977 ·
ARCO Center for the Arts, Los Angeles, 1978

Selected group exhibitions

Studio Coalition, Boston, 1969, 1970 · Museum of Modern
Art, New York City, 1970 · Hayden Gallery, M.I.T., Cambridge, 1971, 1972 · Institute of Contemporary Art, Boston,
1972, 1973 · Fogg Art Museum, Cambridge, 1972 · Balti-
more Museum of Art, 1972 · Hudson River Museum at
Yonkers, New York, 1973 · North Carolina State University, Raleigh, 1973 · The Photographer's Gallery, London,
1974 · Museum of Fine Arts, Boston, 1974 · University of
Alabama, 1975 · Documenta Gallery, Turin, Italy, 1973,
1975 · Vision Gallery, Boston, 1976 · University of Mis-
souri, St. Louis, 1976

Selected publications

Art in America, 1970; *Aperture; Camera 35; Aspen Magazine #9; Popular Photography; Esquire, 1976; Boston
Review of the Arts*

Selected Collections

Museum of Modern Art; Fogg Art Museum; George East-
man House, Rochester; Museum of Fine Arts, Boston;
Virginia Museum of Fine Arts, Richmond; M.I.T.; Vassar
College, Poughkeepsie, New York.

Mr. Friedman's original monoprints are in color and appear on pp. 24 through 27.

JEROME LIEBLING, *Amherst*

Born 1924, New York City
Education: Brooklyn College; Film Workshop, New School
for Social Research, New York City

Jerome Liebling has been a Professor of Film and Photography at Hampshire College in Amherst, Massachusetts, since 1970. He has also taught at Yale University, New Haven, Connecticut; State University of New York at New Paltz; University of Minnesota, Minneapolis; the University Film Study Center Summer Institutes (Massachusetts); Center of the Eye in Aspen, Colorado; and the J.F.K. Institute in Berlin. He is a founding member of the Society for Photographic Education.

Selected solo exhibitions

Walker Art Center, Minneapolis, 1950 · George Eastman House, Rochester, New York, 1957 · Minneapolis Institute of Art, 1958, 1963 · Museum of Modern Art, New York City, 1963 · Hampshire College, 1972 · Union College, Schenectady, New York, 1975 · Vision Gallery, Boston, 1977

Selected group exhibitions

Museum of Modern Art, 1963 · George Eastman House, 1963 · Expo 67, Montreal, 1967 · University of New Hampshire, Durham, 1968 · U.C.L.A. Art Gallery, 1968 · Pennsylvania State University Gallery, University Park, 1972 · Fred S. Wight Gallery, U.C.L.A., 1976 · 1976 Guggenheim Photographers, College V, Santa Cruz, California, 1976 · Cornell University, Ithaca, New York, 1976 · University of Massachusetts, Amherst, 1977 · New York Historical Society, New York City, 1978 · Sam Wagstaff Collection, Corcoran Gallery of Art, Washington, D. C., 1978 · Museum of Fine Arts, Boston, 1978

Selected publications

Aperture, 1956; *Massachusetts Review*, 1957, 1972; *Contemporary Photography*, 1963; *The Face of Minneapolis*, 1966; *Time-Life Documentary Photography*, 1972; *Faces: A Narrative History of the Portrait in Photography*, 1977; *Photographs, Sheldon Memorial Art Gallery Collection*, University of Nebraska, 1977; *A Book of Photographs from the Samuel Wagstaff Collection*, 1978; *Aperture*, 1978.

Selected collections

Museum of Fine Arts, Boston; Museum of Modern Art; George Eastman House; Center for Photography, University of Arizona, Tucson; Library of Congress; Fogg Art Museum; Yale University Art Gallery; U.C.L.A. Art Gallery; Minneapolis Institute of Art; private collections.

Awards, prizes

National Endowment for the Arts Photography Fellowship, 1972; Guggenheim Photography Fellowship, 1976; several awards for films.

Mr. Liebling's black-and-white photographs appear on pp. 28 through 31.

WENDY MACNEIL, *Lincoln*

Born 1943, Boston
Education: Smith College, B.A.; Harvard University,
M.A.T.; studied for two years as a special student with
Minor White, M.I.T., Cambridge.

Wendy MacNeil has been an Assistant Professor at Wellesley College, Massachusetts, since 1973. She has also taught
at the Rhode Island School of Design, Providence. She
has published a book of photographs, *Haymarket,* and is
finishing her second book, *Biographical Fragments,* com-
bining photographs and oral histories.

Selected solo exhibitions

Addison Gallery of American Art, Andover, Massachu-
setts, 1971, 1976 · Carl Siembab Gallery, Boston, 1972 ·
Half Moon Gallery, London, 1972 · Baldwin Street Gallery,
Toronto, 1973 · ASA Gallery, University of New Mexico,
Albuquerque, 1974 · M.I.T. Creative Photography Gallery,
Cambridge, 1975 · Photographic Eye Gallery, Cambridge,
1977

Selected group exhibitions

M.I.T. Creative Photography Gallery, 1969 · Institute of
Contemporary Art, Boston, 1972 · Smith College, North-
ampton, Massachusetts, 1974 · Museum of Fine Arts, Bos-
ton, 1974, 1978 · Fashion Institute of Technology, New
York City, 1976 · Witkin Gallery, New York City, 1976 ·
Womanspace, Boulder, Colorado, 1976 · Rhode Island
School of Design, 1977 · University of New Hampshire,
Durham, 1977 · Worcester Art Museum, Massachusetts,
1977

Selected publications

Aperture, 1974; *Massachusetts Review,* 1974; *The Photographer's Choice,* 1976; *Women See Women,* 1976; *Ms.
Magazine; Afterimage; Popular Photography.*

Selected collections

Museum of Fine Arts, Boston; Addison Gallery of American Art; University of Massachusetts, Amherst.

Awards, prizes

AIGA 50 Books of the Year Award, 1970, for *Haymarket,*
M.I.T. Press; Guggenheim Photography Fellowship, 1973;
National Endowment for the Arts Photography Fellow-
ship, 1974, 1978.

Ms. MacNeil's original prints are in platinum and appear
on pp. 32 through 35.

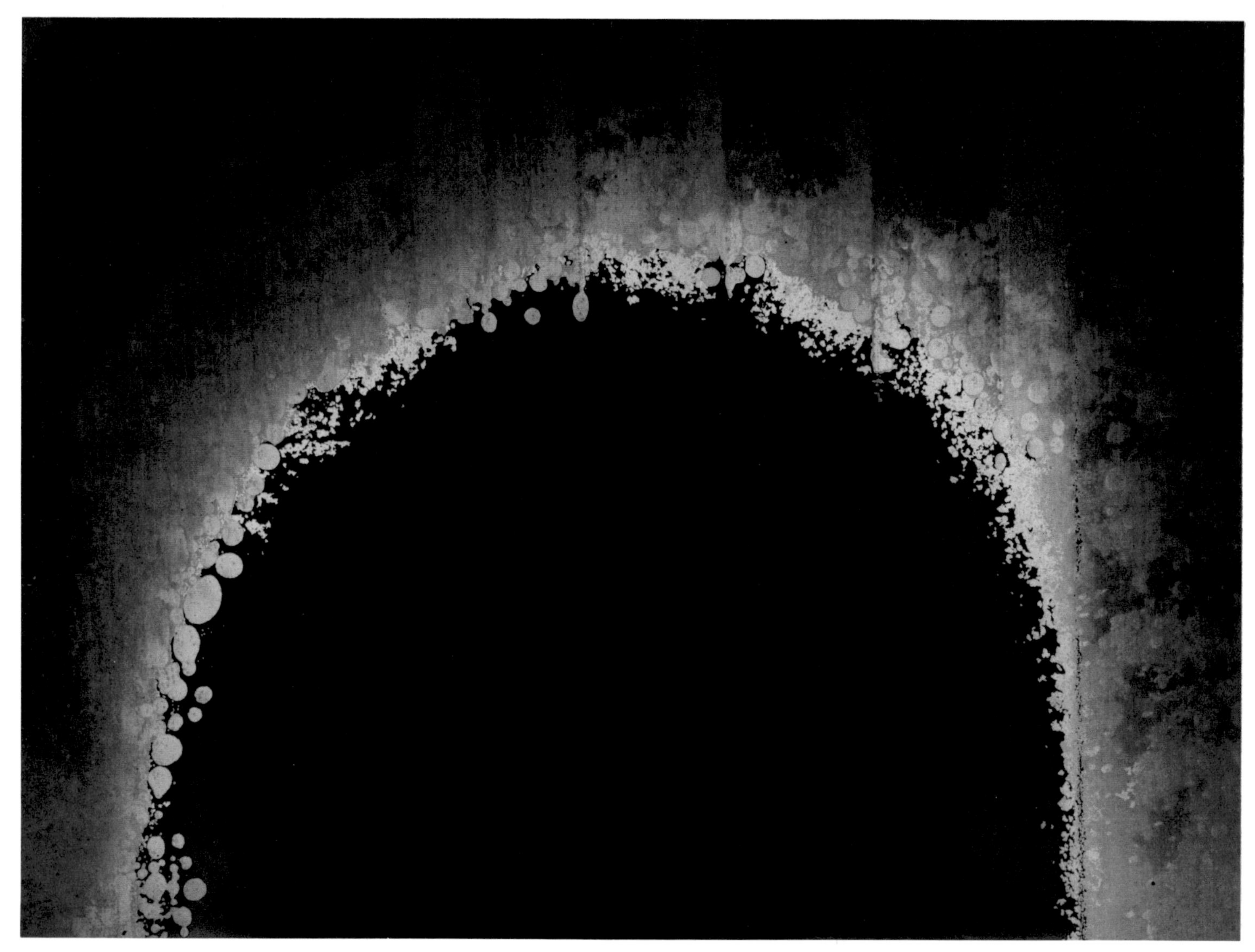

CARL CHIARENZA · *Somerville #12, 1975*

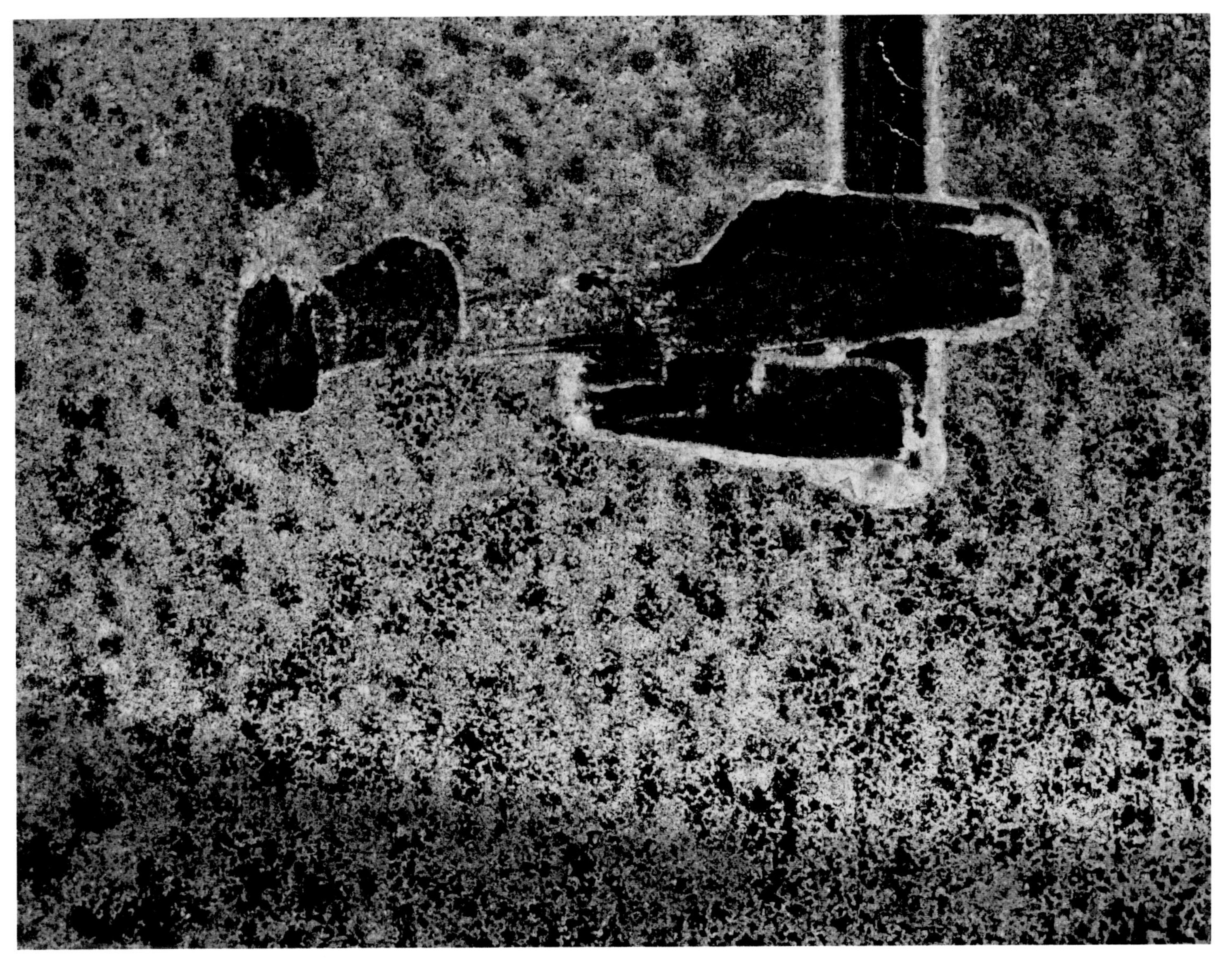

Charlestown #53, 1976 · CARL CHIARENZA

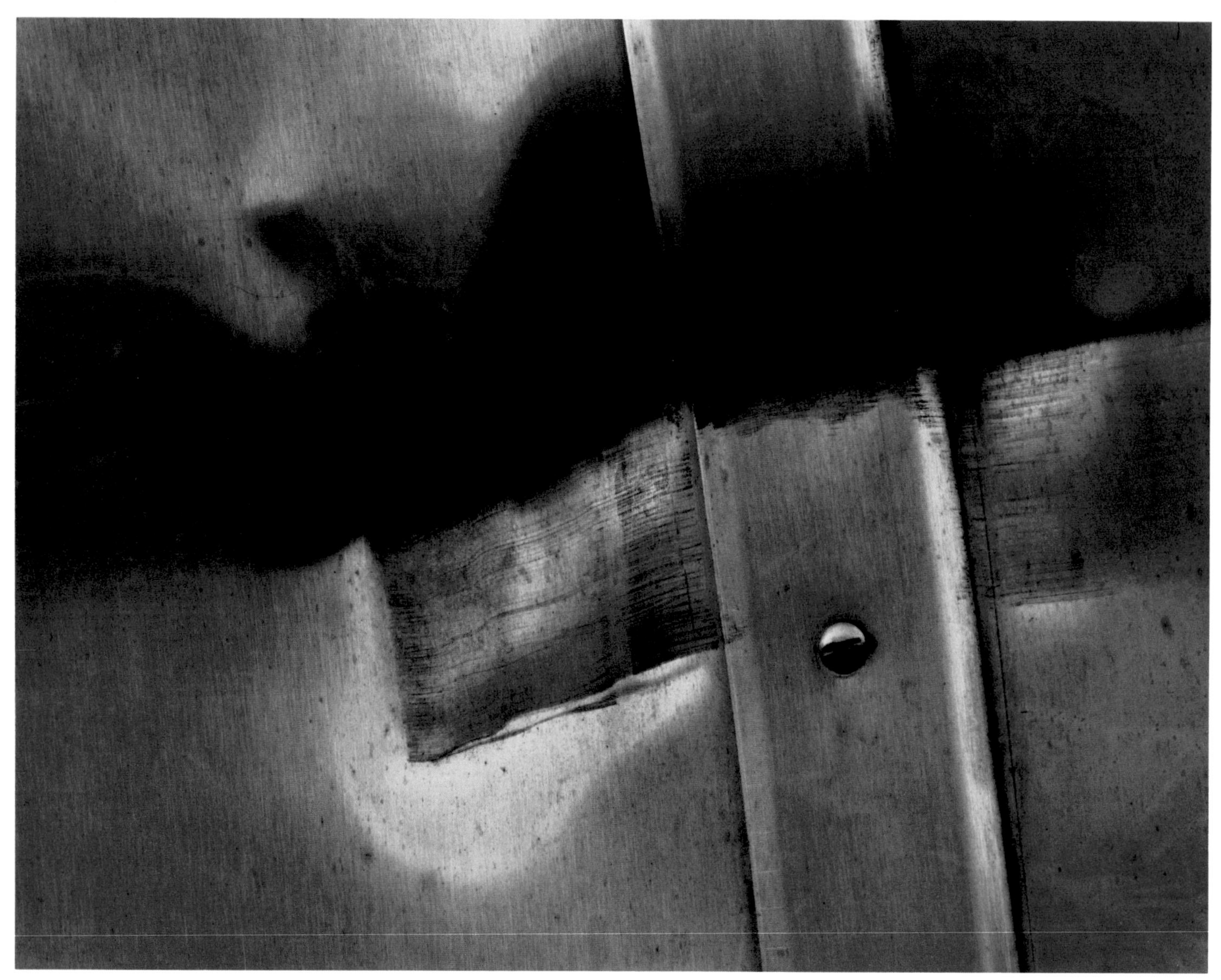

CARL CHIARENZA · *Somerville #10, 1976*

18

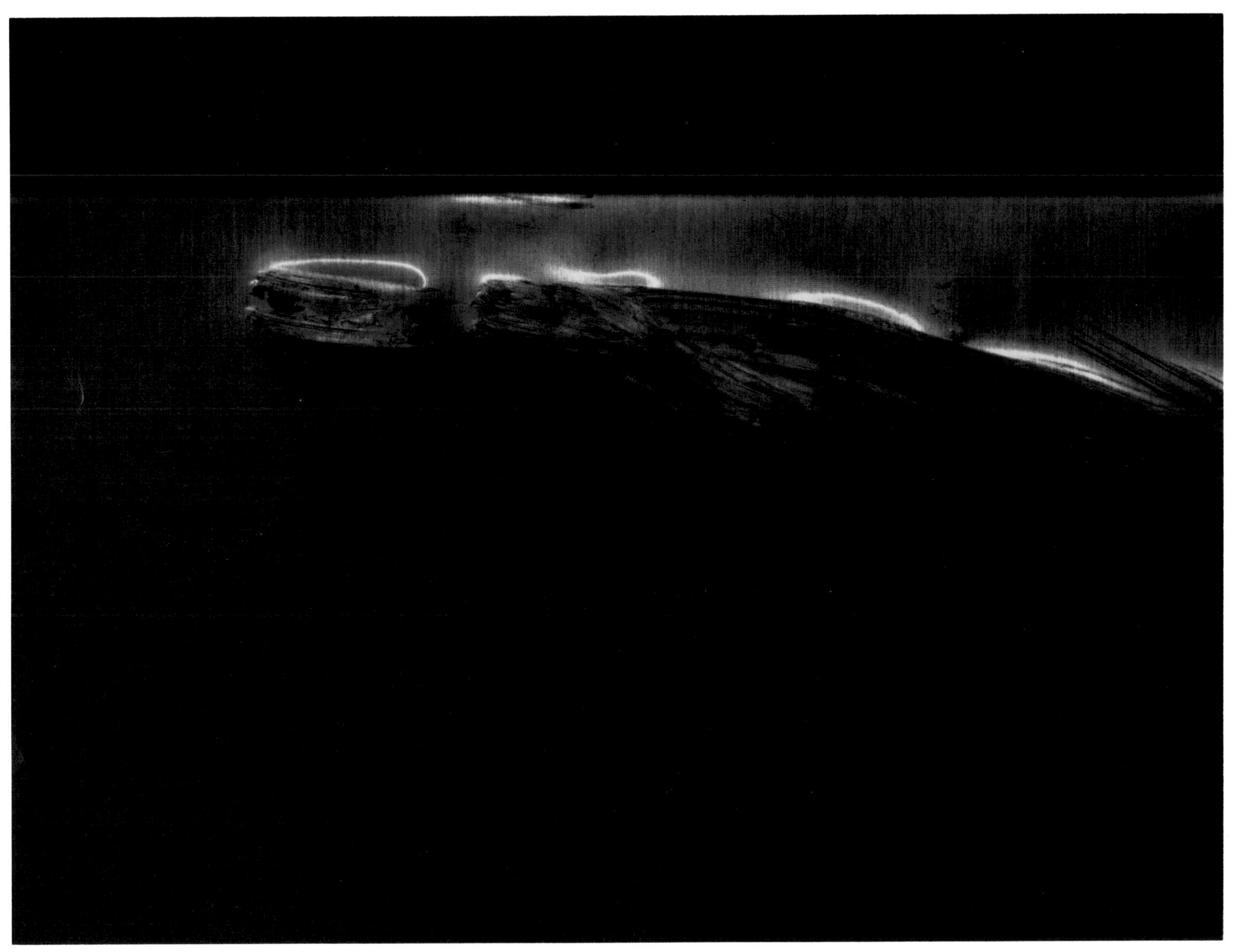

Somerville #21, 1976 · CARL CHIARENZA

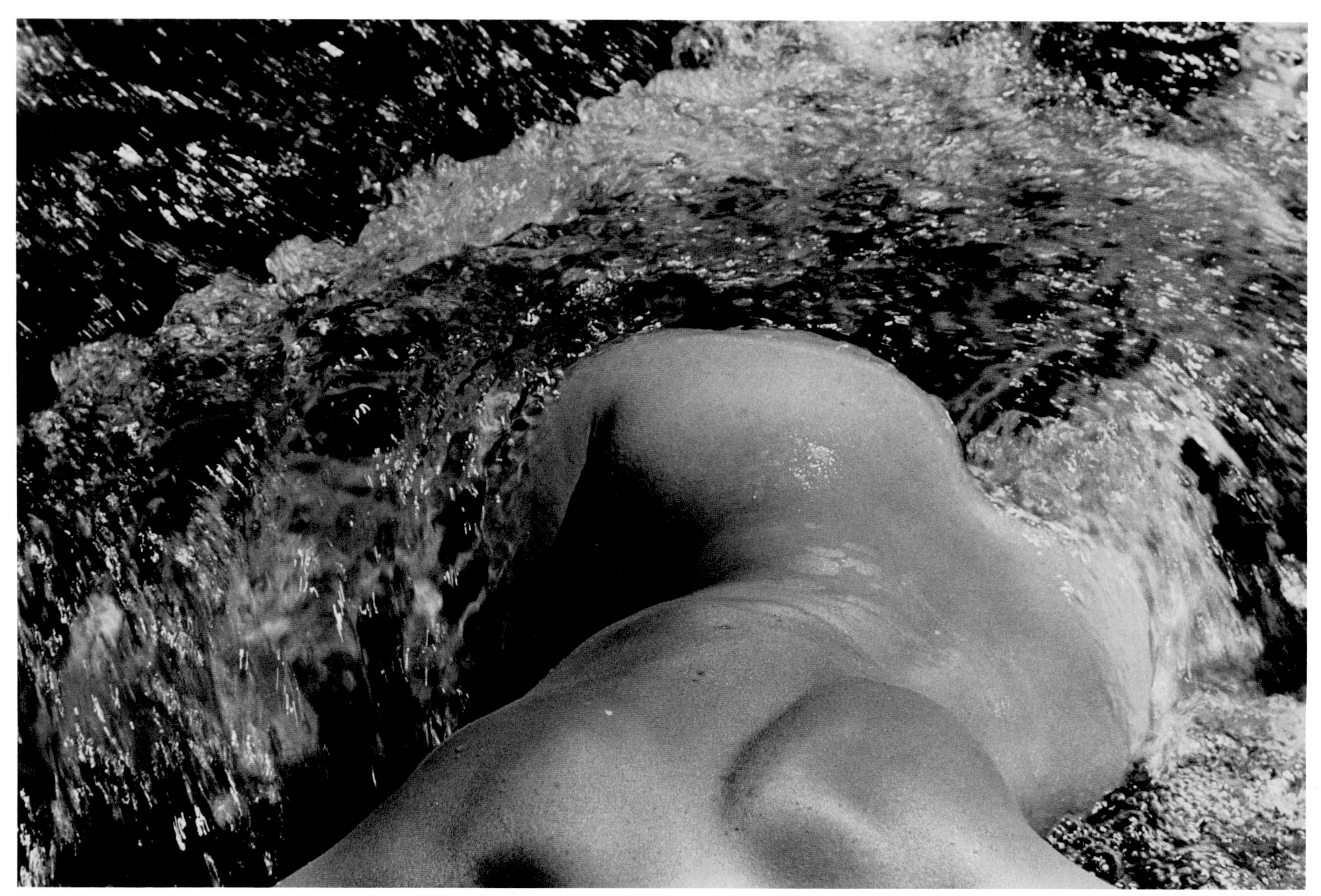

CHRIS ENOS · *1975*

20

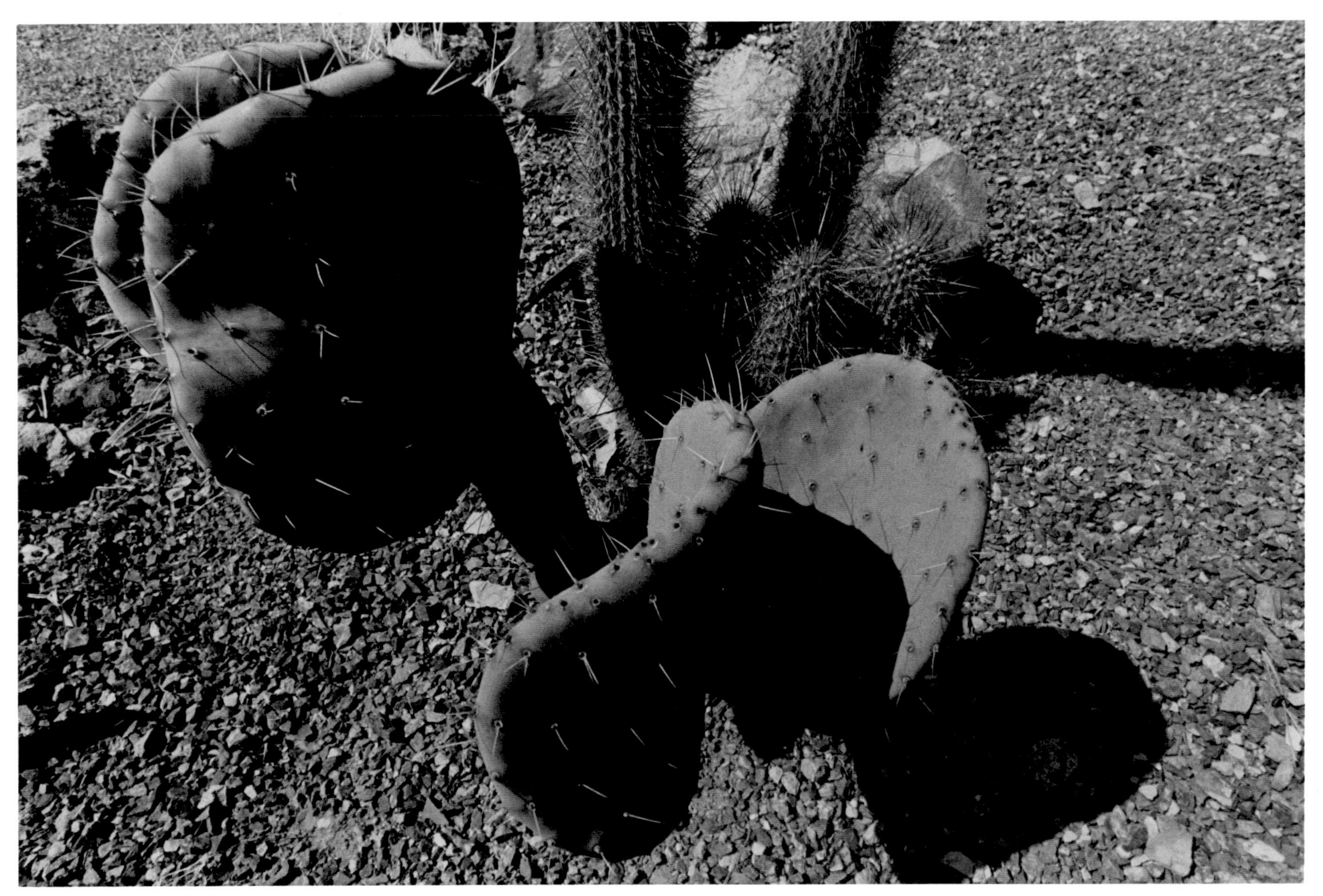

1977 · CHRIS ENOS

21

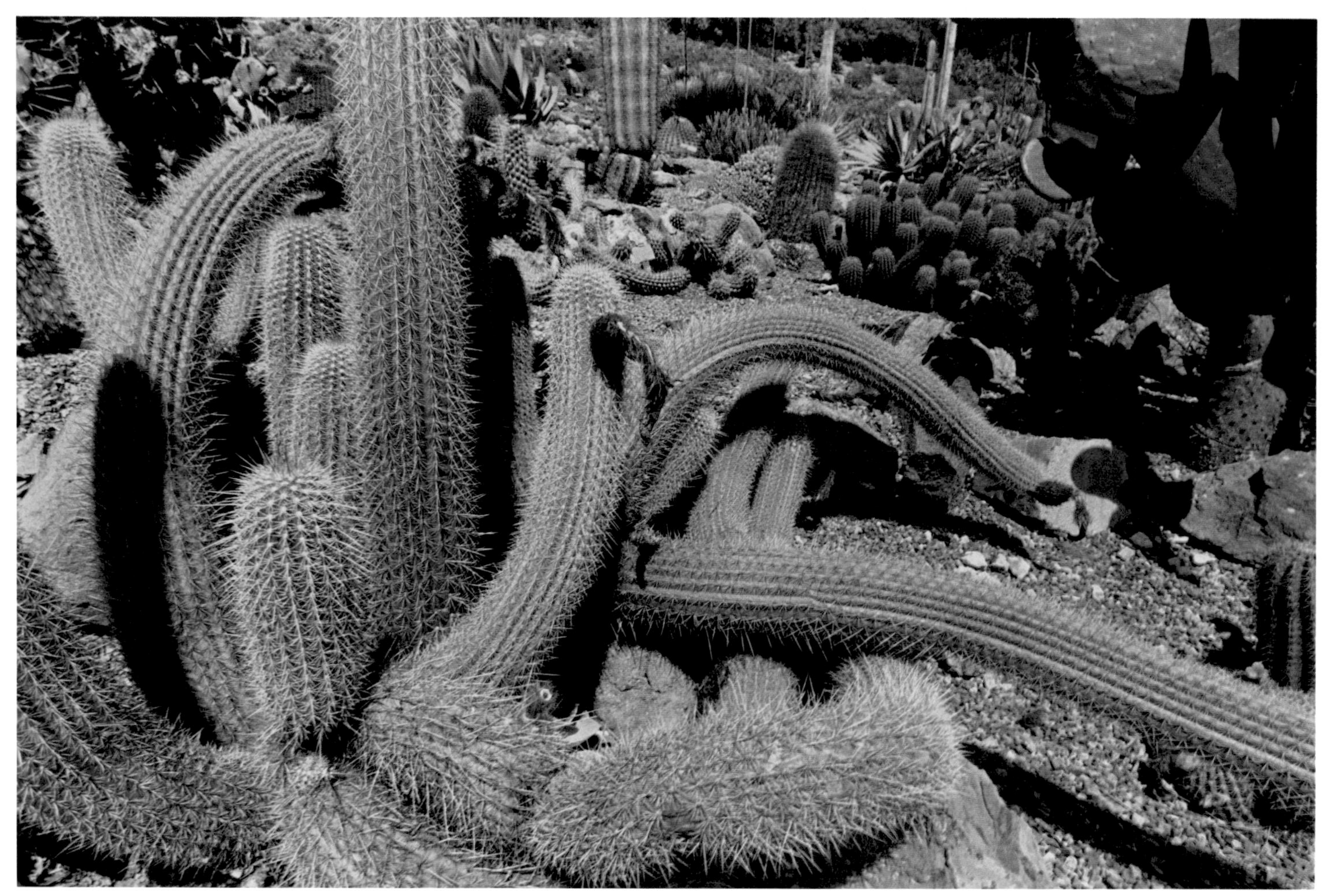

CHRIS ENOS · 1977

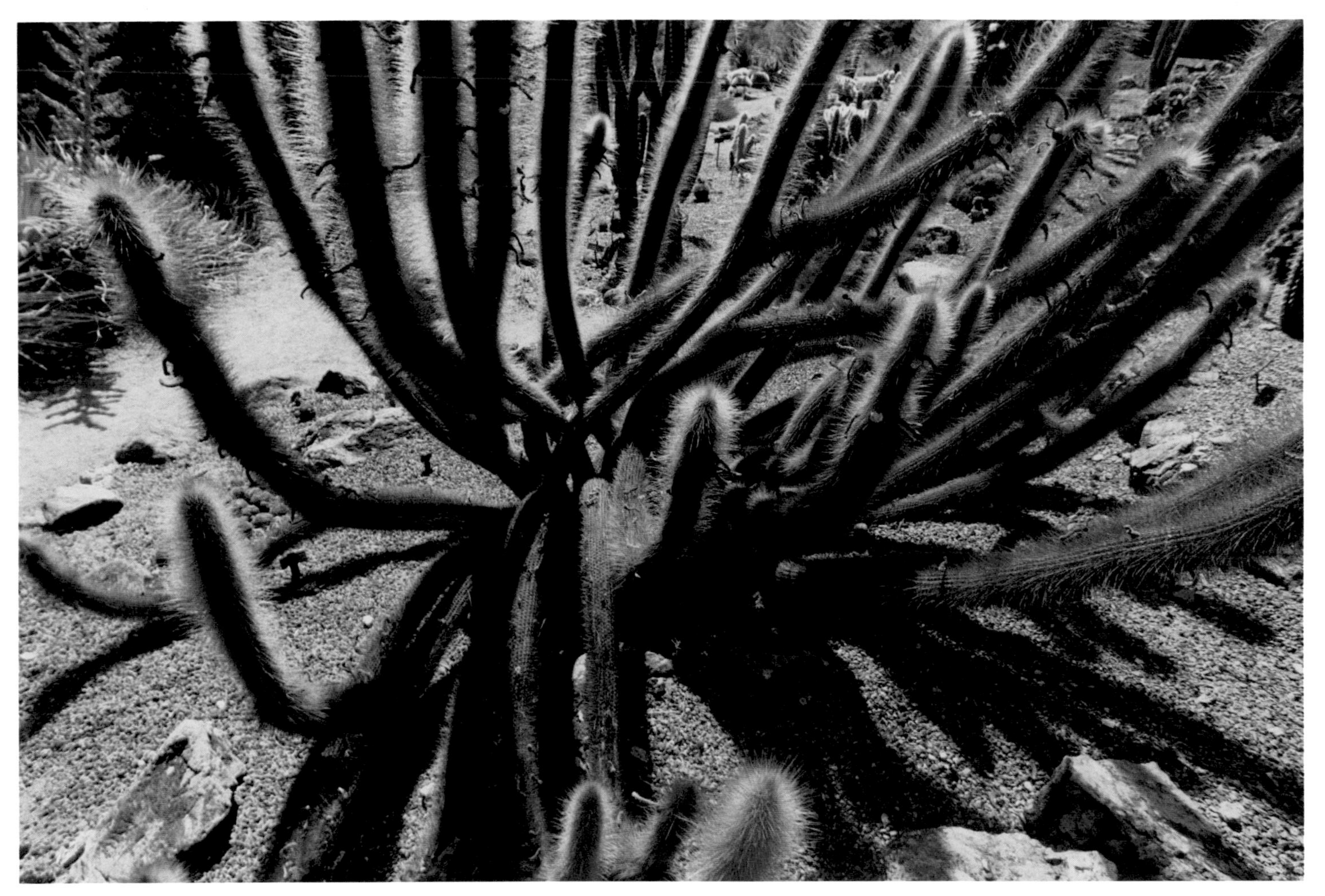

1977 · CHRIS ENOS

23

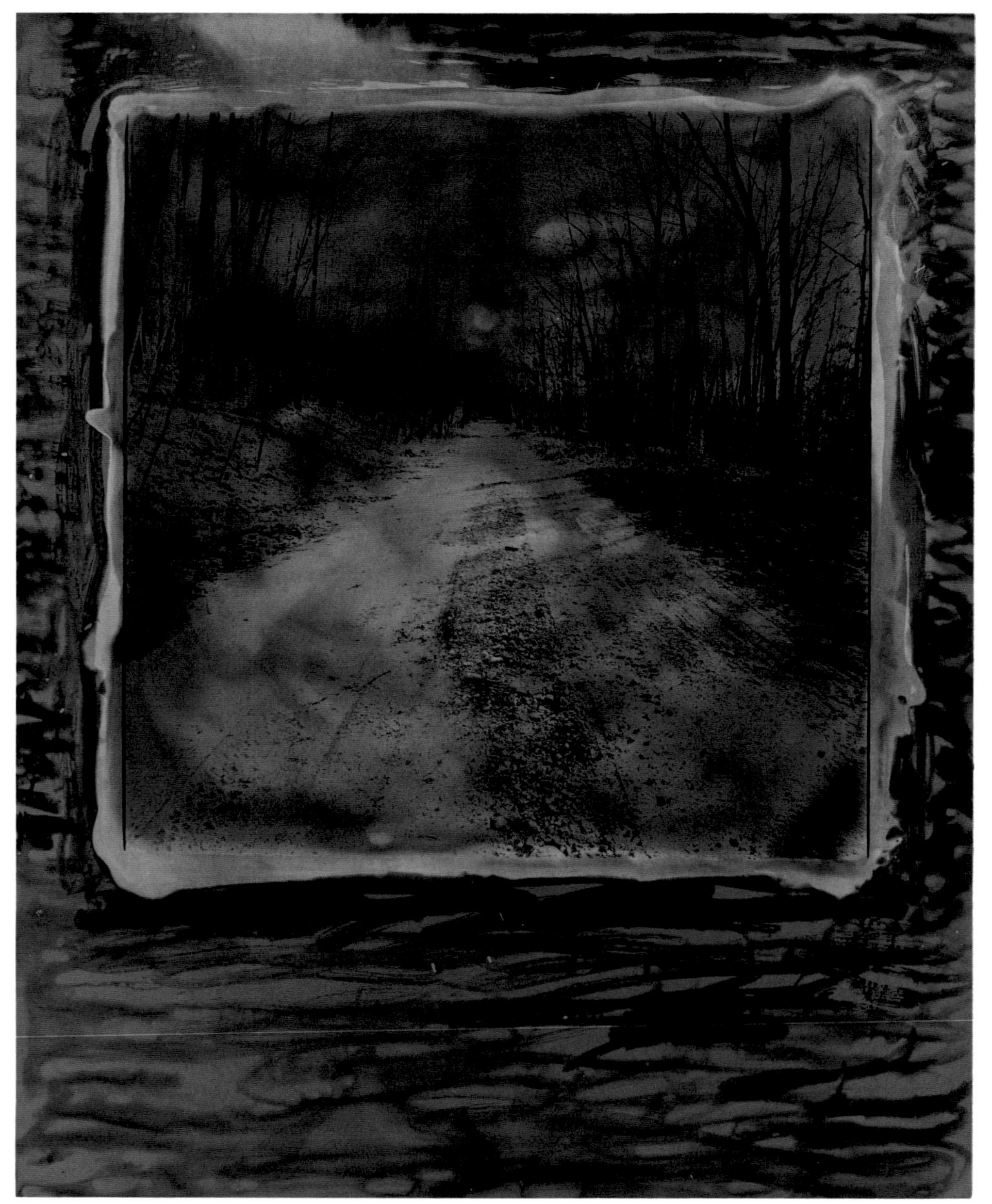

BENNO FRIEDMAN · *1974*

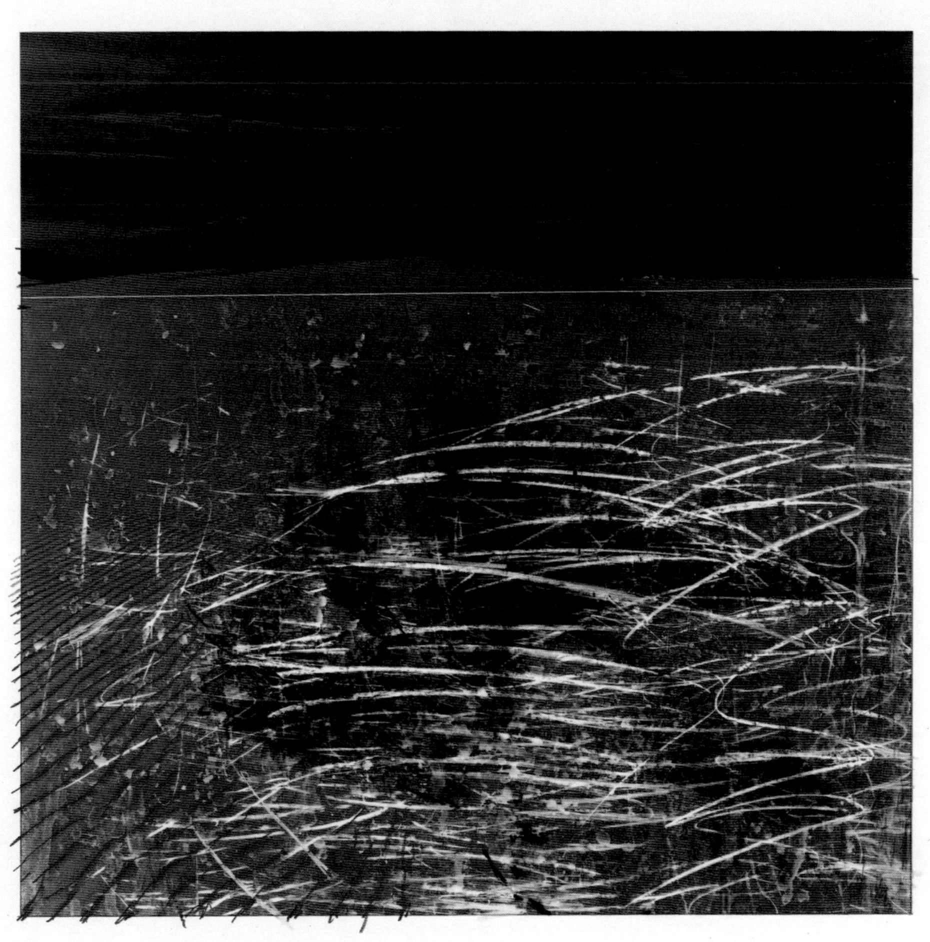

1976 · BENNO FRIEDMAN

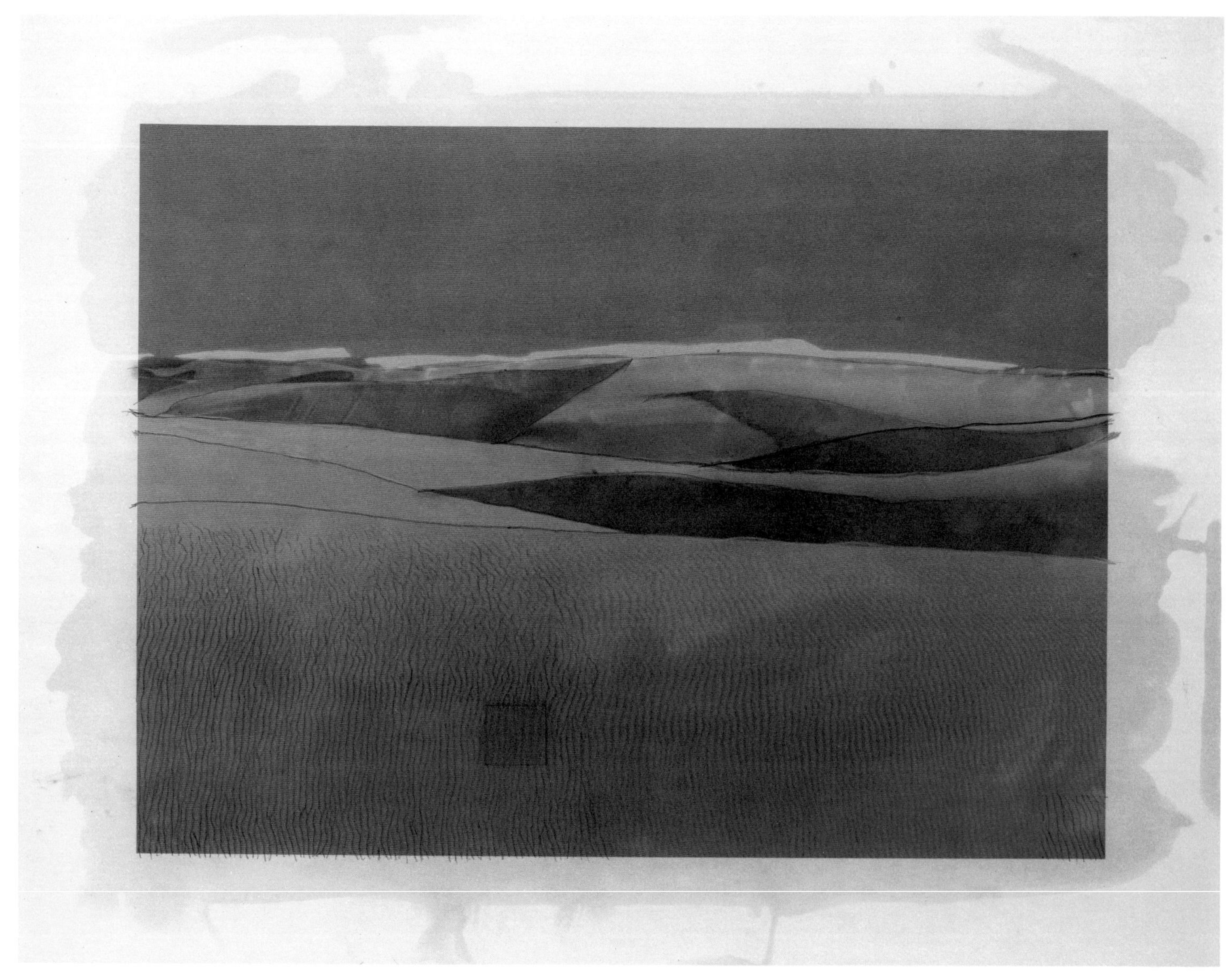

BENNO FRIEDMAN · *1976*

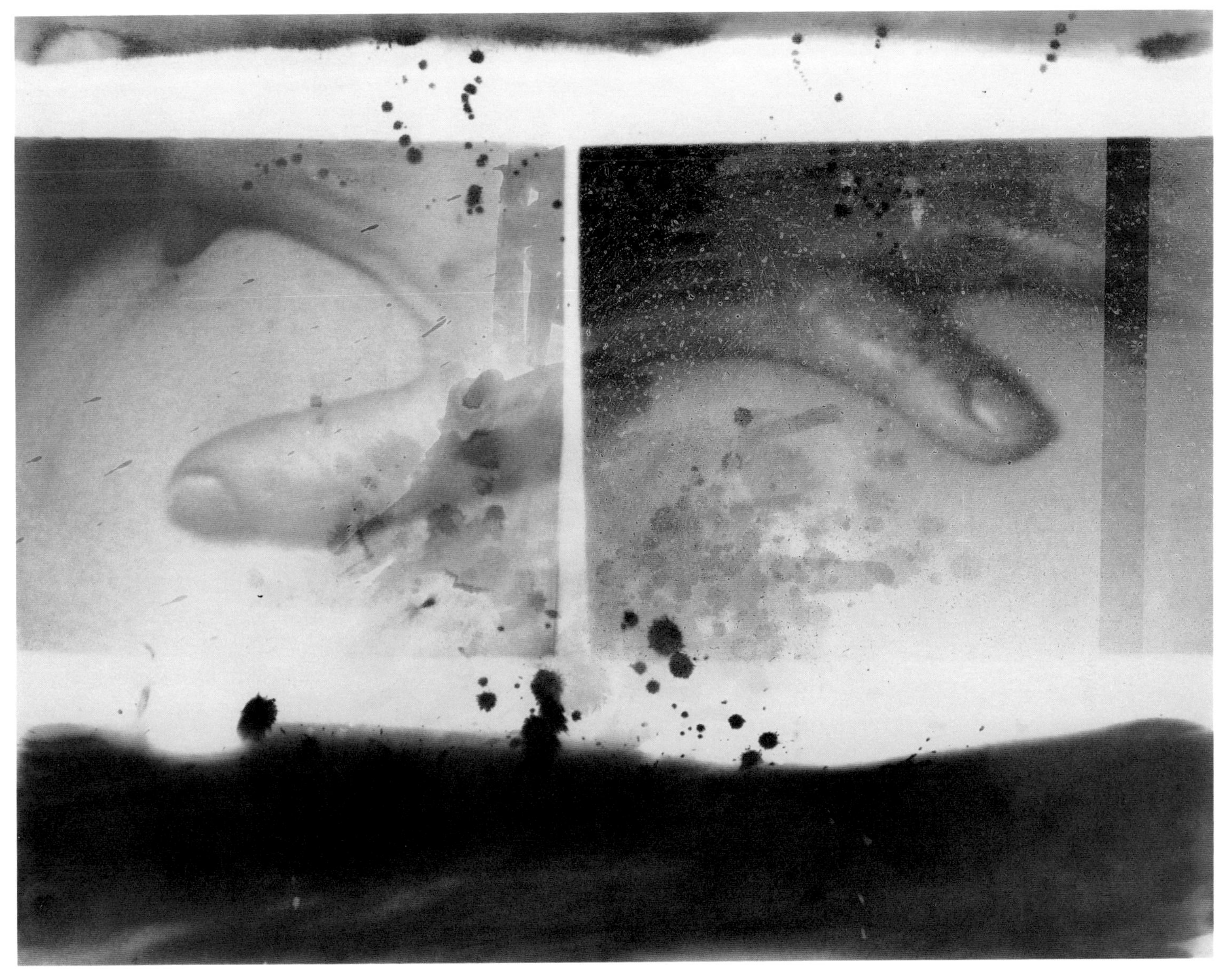

1974 · BENNO FRIEDMAN

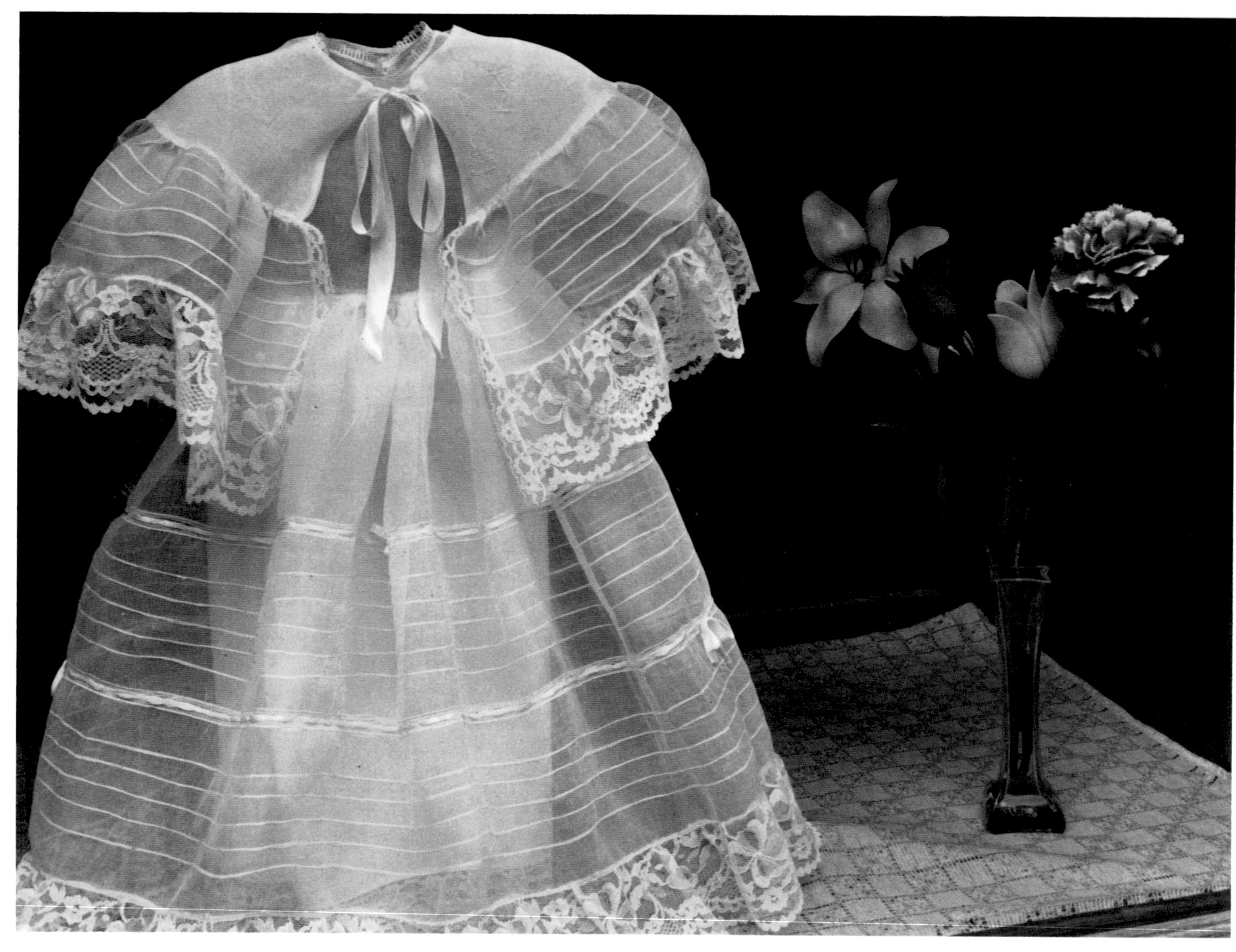

JEROME LIEBLING · *Confirmation Dress, Malaga, Spain, 1967*

28

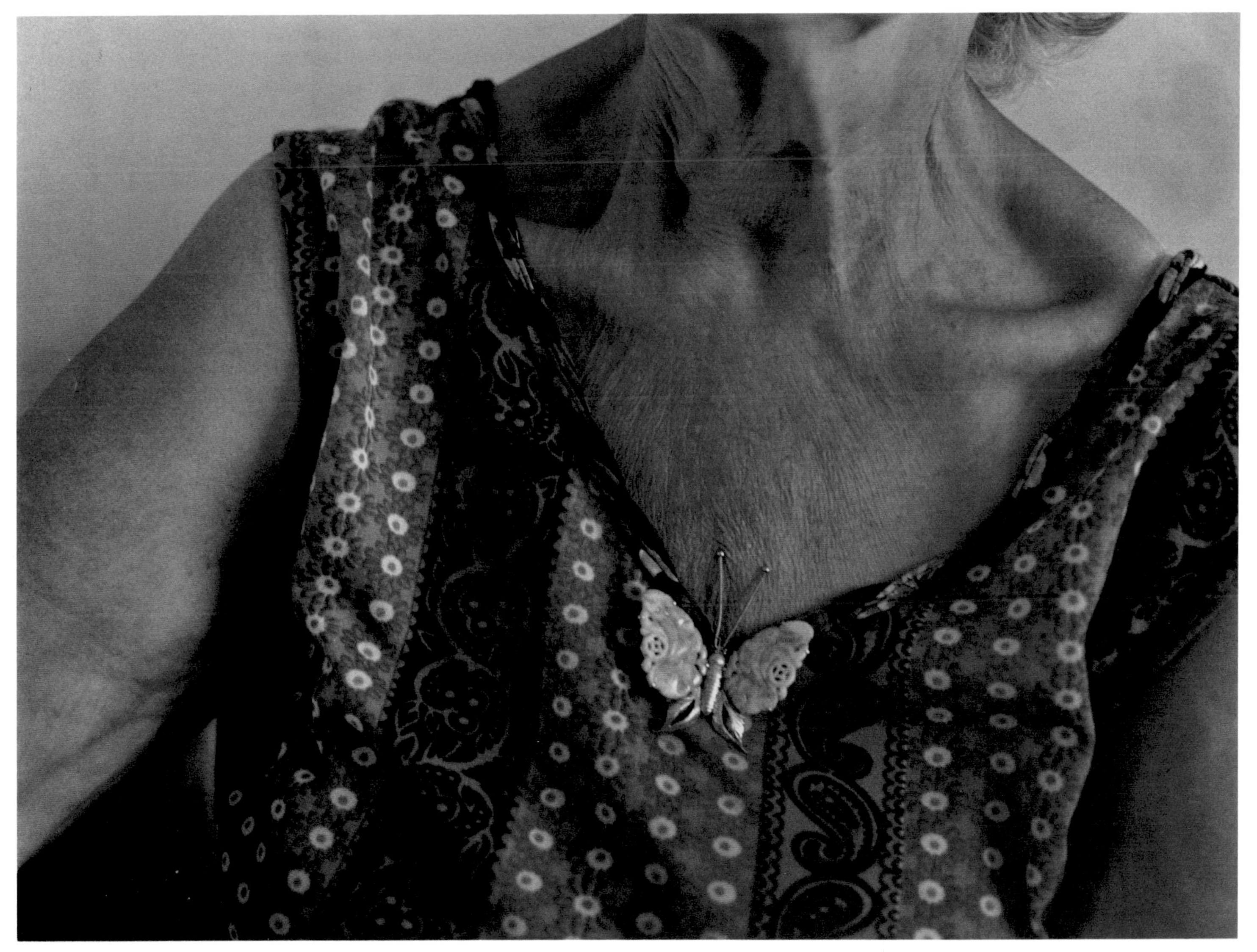

Sarah, 1977 · JEROME LIEBLING

29

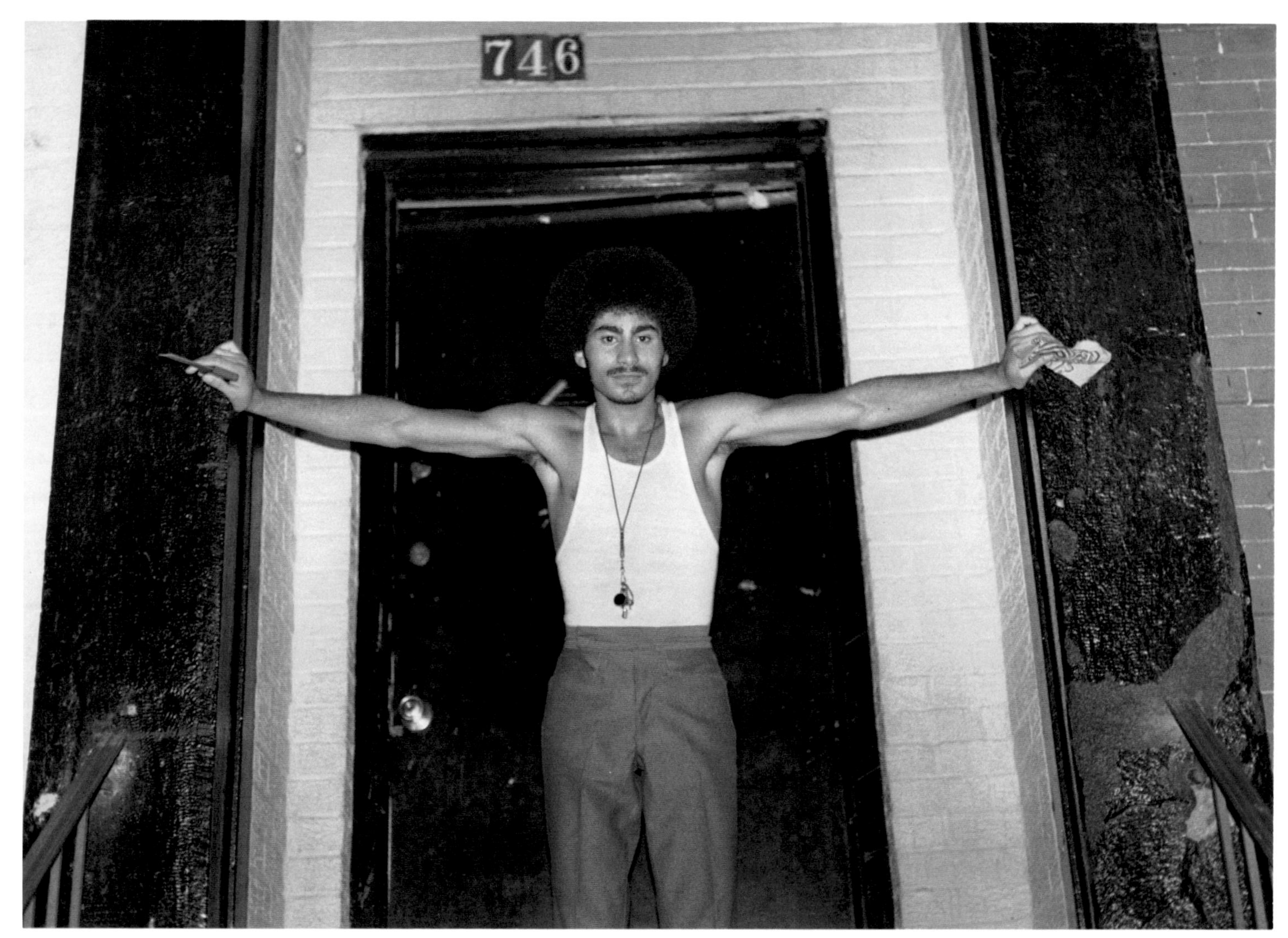

JEROME LIEBLING · *Avenue D, New York City, 1977*

30

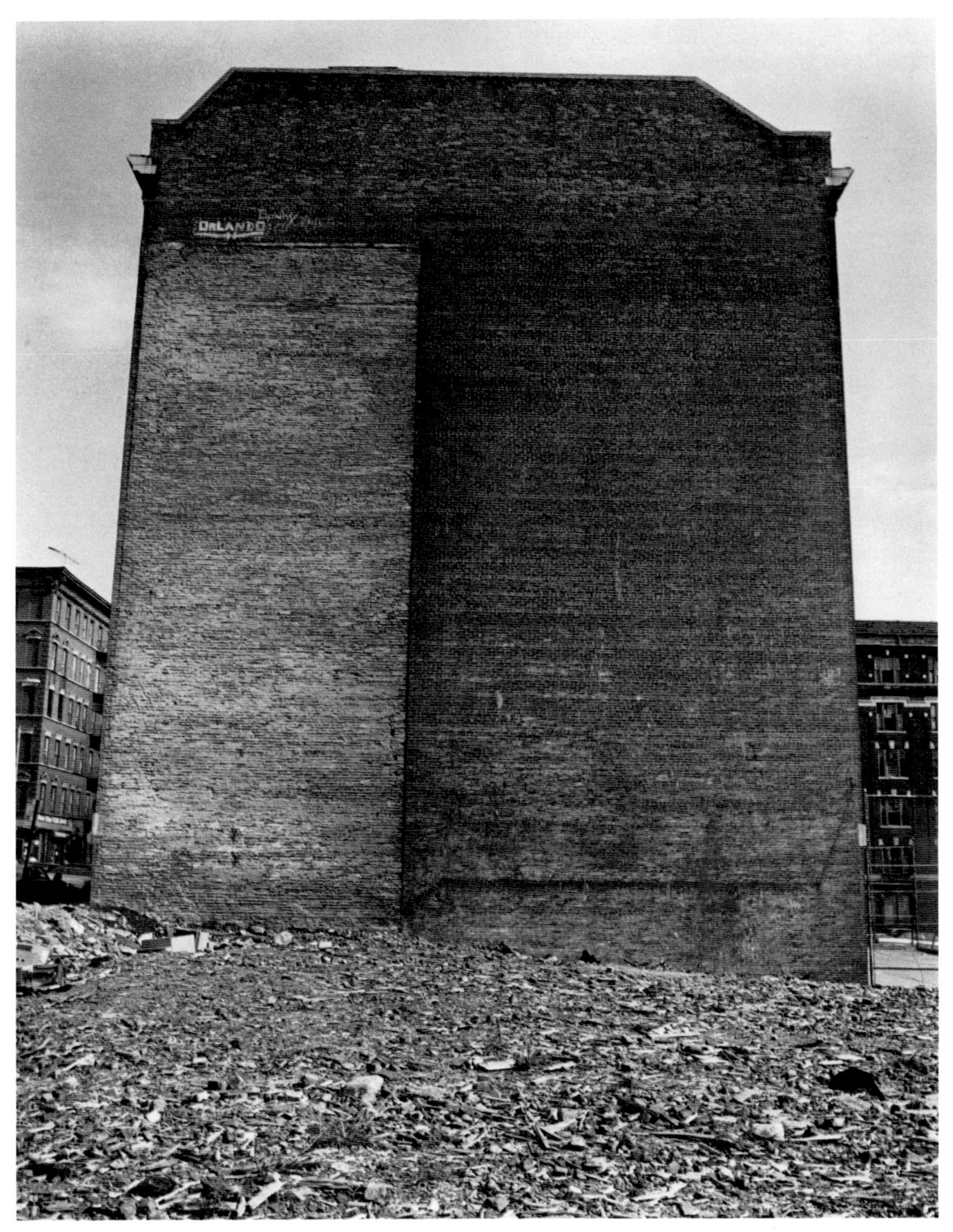

South Bronx,
New York City, 1977

JEROME LIEBLING

31

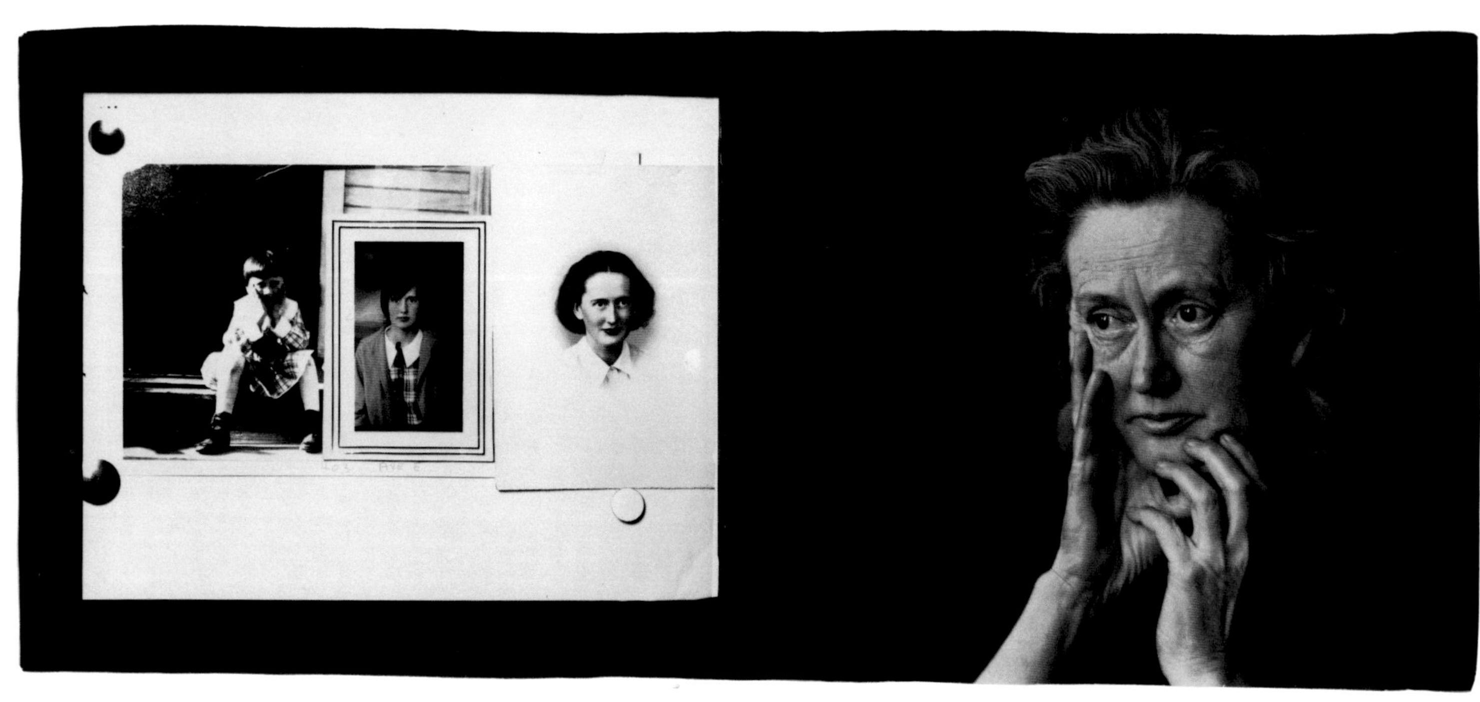

WENDY MACNEIL · *Virginia Powell, 1975*

32

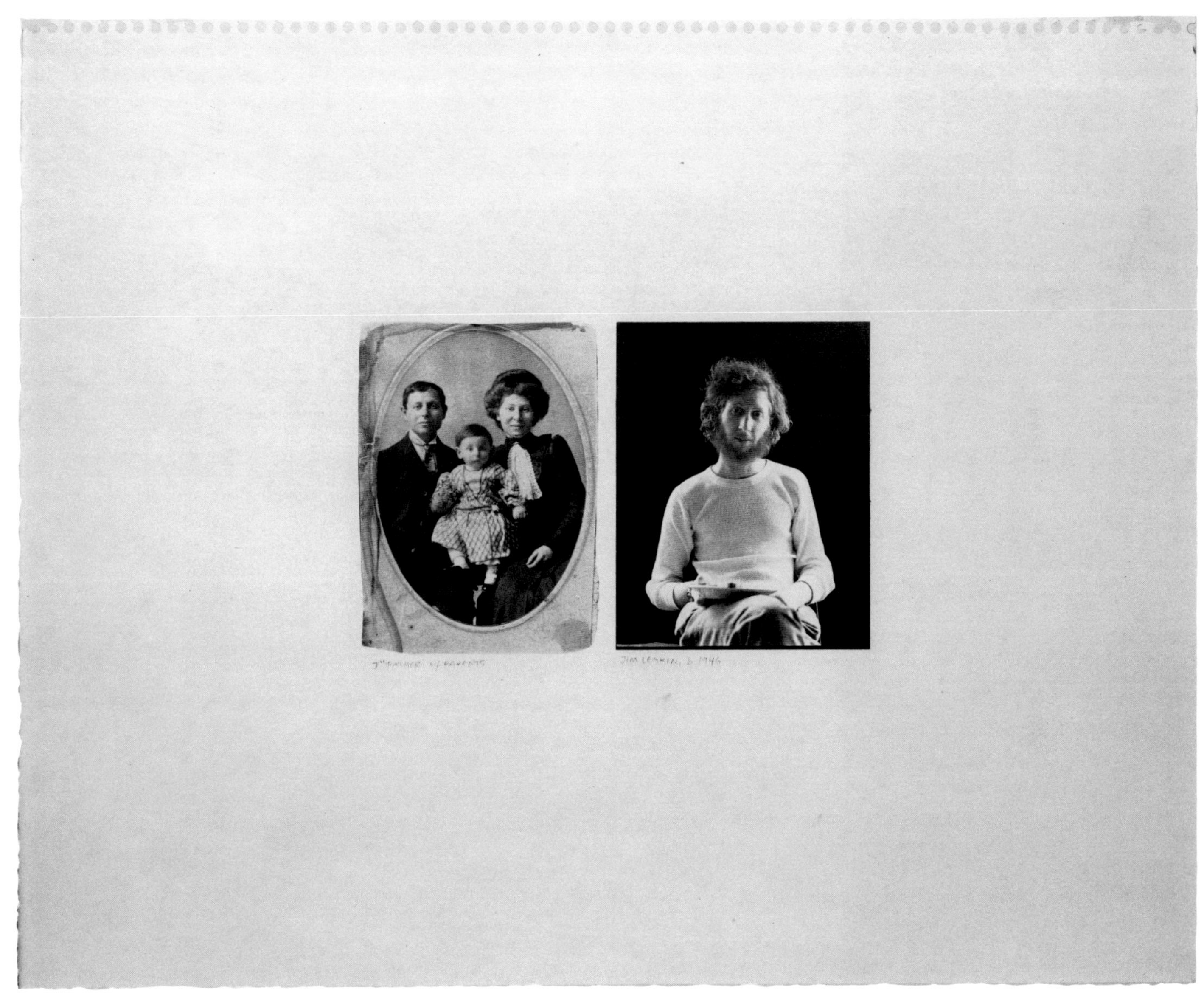

Jim Lemkin, with Father and Grandparents, 1976 · WENDY MACNEIL

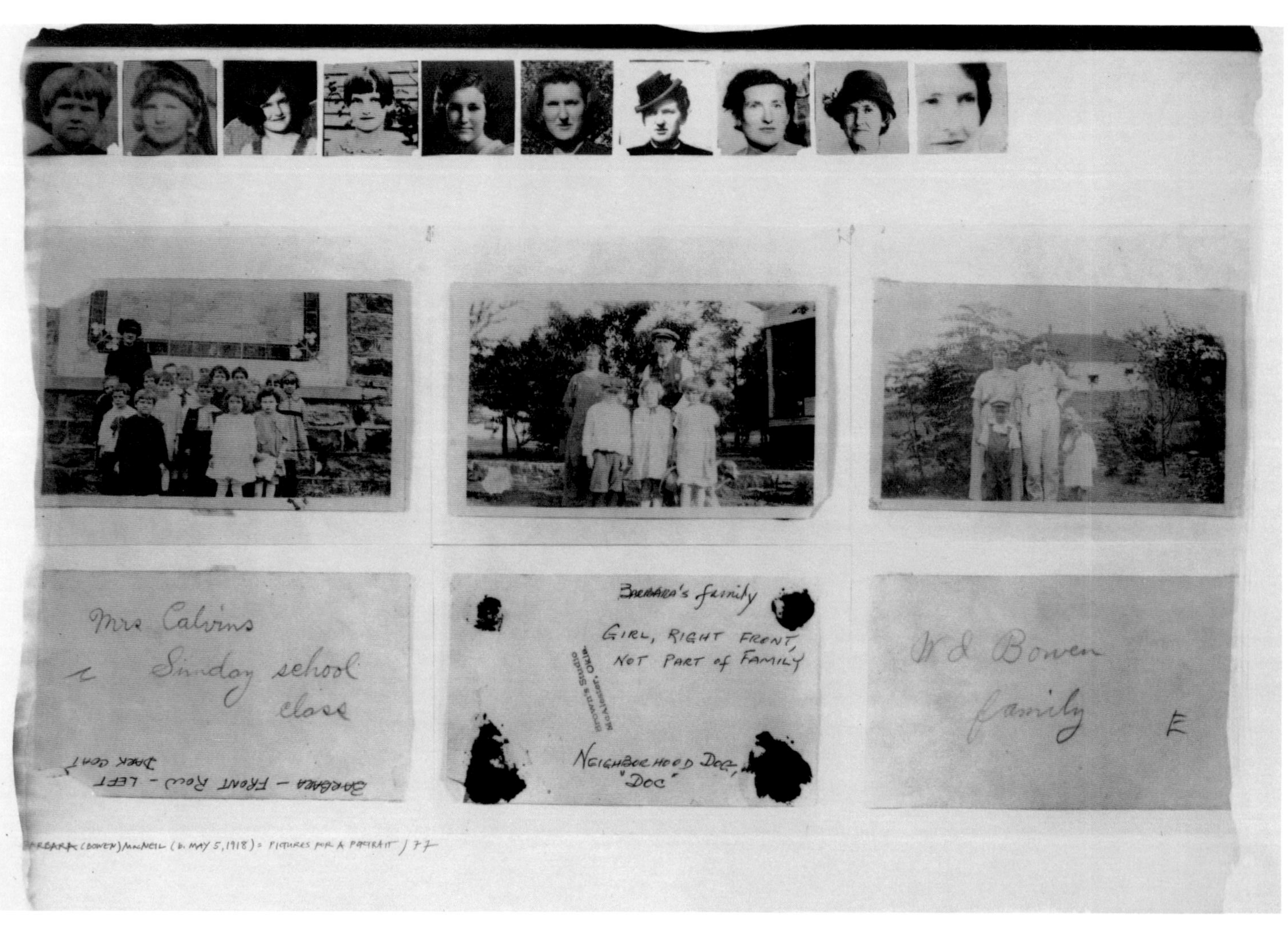

WENDY MACNEIL · *Barbara MacNeil, Pictures for a Portrait, 1977*

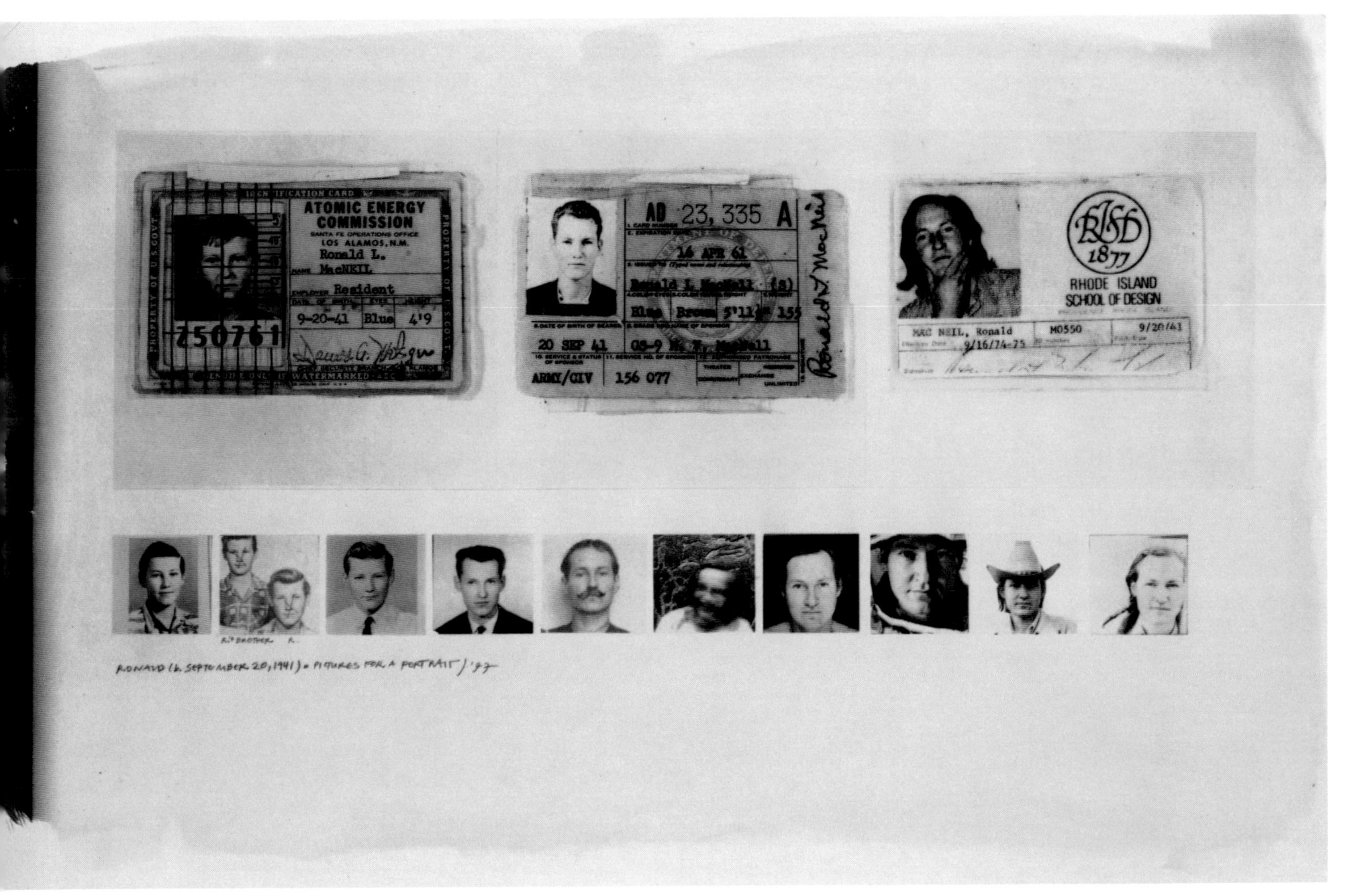

Ronald MacNeil, Pictures for a Portrait, 1977 · WENDY MACNEIL

1976 Fellowship Recipients
Biographies

The panelists were CHARLES HARBUTT, WILLIAM LARSON and BARBARA MORGAN. The six recipients were selected from 305 applicants.

STEPHEN R. ELSTON, *Brookline*

Born 1948, New Haven, Connecticut
Education: Yale University, B.A.; Goddard College, M.A.

Stephen Elston teaches printmaking and experimental photography at the New England School of Photography, Boston. He also lectures on photography at Northeastern University, Boston.

Solo exhibitions

Northeastern University Art Gallery, 1976 · Exposure Gallery, Wellfleet, Massachusetts 1977

Selected group exhibitions

Imageworks, Cambridge, 1973, 1974, 1975 · Boston Center for the Arts, 1975 · New England School of Photography, 1975 · Focus Gallery, San Francisco, 1975 · First Light Exhibition, Eureka, California, 1975 · Northeastern University, 1975 · Enjay Gallery, Boston, 1977 · Boston College,

1977 · M.I.T. Creative Photography Gallery, Cambridge, 1977

Mr. Elston's original work is in color, produced by pigments with the gum bichromate process; the gum emulsion was applied with an airbrush. He is now making multicolored oil prints. His prints appear on pp. 40 through 43.

CHESTER MICHALIK, *Rehoboth*

Born 1935, Holyoke, Massachusetts
Education: Massachusetts College of Art, B.S.; Boston University, M.F.A.

Chester Michalik is Associate Professor of Film Studies at the Rhode Island School of Design, Providence, at which he has taught since 1965. He has also taught at Imageworks in Cambridge, and the Massachusetts College of Art, Boston.

Selected solo exhibitions

University of New Hampshire, Durham, 1965 · Carl Siembab Gallery, Boston, 1970, 1975, 1977 · Rochester Institute of Technology, New York, 1971 · Cronin Gallery, Houston, Texas, 1976 · Quinacqua Limited Gallery, Washington, D. C., 1977

Selected group exhibitions

Gallery 216, New York City, 1965 · M.I.T., Cambridge, 1965 · Worcester Art Museum, Massachusetts, 1968 · International Museum of Photography, Rochester, 1968 · Witkin Gallery, New York City, 1969 · Amon Carter Museum of Art, Fort Worth, Texas, 1969 · Museum of Fine Arts, Boston, 1969 · Minneapolis Institute of Art, 1969 · Institute of Contemporary Art, Boston, 1972 · Middlebury College, Vermont, 1972 · Museum of Art, Houston, Texas, 1977 · Museum of Fine Arts, Boston, 1978

Publications

Photography, London, England; *Boston Magazine*; *Journal of Popular Culture.*

Selected collections

Worcester Art Museum; Visual Studies Workshop, Rochester; International Museum of Photography, Rochester; Wellesley College, Massachusetts; Kansas City Museum of Art, Kansas; Art Institute of Chicago; Rhode Island School of Design; Arts Museum, Toronto.

Awards, prizes

Fulbright Fellowship, 1967

Mr. Michalik's black-and-white photographs appear on pp. 44 through 47.

THOMAS J. PETIT, *Taunton*

Born 1942, Doylestown, Ohio
Education: Kent State University, B.S.; Rochester Institute of Technology, M.F.A.

Thomas Petit teaches a variety of color photography courses at the New England School of Photography, Boston. He has also worked as a free-lance photographer. Recently he has been investigating small-town photography in the United States at the turn of the century, working with his own collection of 2,500 glass negatives from the 1895-1920 period.

Selected solo exhibitions

Rochester Institute of Technology, New York, 1975 (two exhibitions) · Franklinville, New York, 1976 · Gallery One, New England School of Photography, 1977

Selected group exhibitions

Syracuse University, New York, 1973 · Rochester Institute

of Technology, 1973, 1974, 1975 · New England School of Photography, 1975, 1977 · Enjay Gallery, Boston, 1977

Mr. Petit's original photographs are in color and were made with an Arrow camera (Diana class). His photographs appear on pp. 48 through 51.

NANCY RANKIN, *Arlington*

Born 1944, Woonsocket, Rhode Island
Education: Sarah Lawrence College, B.A.; Boston University School of Social Work, M.S.W.; Advanced Workshops at the New England School of Photography and Project, Inc., Cambridge.

Nancy Rankin teaches Women's Studies at the Winsor School in Boston. The photographs reproduced in this book are taken from a six-year study of adolescent girls.

Solo exhibition

Cape Split Place, South Addison, Maine, 1978

Group exhibitions

Panopticon Gallery, Boston, 1976 · Enjay Gallery, Boston, 1977

Ms. Rankin's black-and-white photographs appear on pp. 52 through 55.

LAUREN SHAW, *Arlington*

Born 1946, Atlanta, Georgia
Education: Georgia State University, B.V.A.; Rhode Island School of Design, M.F.A.

Lauren Shaw, Assistant Professor in Fine Arts, teaches photography at Emerson College, Boston, at which she has taught since 1972. She has also taught photographic workshops at Apeiron, Millertown, New York, and at the Essex Workshop, Essex, Massachusetts.

Solo exhibitions

Vernon Court Junior College, Newport, Rhode Island, 1971 · Panopticon Gallery, Boston, 1974 · Enjay Gallery, Boston, 1975 · CEPA Gallery, Buffalo, New York, 1977

Selected group exhibitions

Rhode Island School of Design, Providence, 1972 · Project, Inc., Cambridge, 1972 · Perception Gallery, Montreal, 1972 · Harvard University, Cambridge, 1974 · Apeiron Workshops, 1975 · Wheelock College, Boston, 1976 ·

Fogg Art Museum, Cambridge, 1976 · M.I.T. Creative Photography Gallery, Cambridge, 1977 (two-person) · Enjay Gallery, 1977 · Hayden Gallery, M.I.T., 1978

Publications

Foreword Magazine, 1972; *Popular Photography,* 1973; *Ms. Magazine,* 1976; *Women See Women,* 1976.

Collections

Fogg Art Museum; Wellesley College; Apeiron Workshops; private collections.

Ms. Shaw's original black-and-white prints, which are selenium-toned, appear on pp. 56 through 59.

JIM STONE, *Cambridge*

Born 1947, Los Angeles, California
Education: M.I.T., S.B.; Rhode Island School of Design, M.F.A.

Jim Stone teaches photography at Boston College and the Rhode Island School of Design, Providence. He was an artist-in-residence for the Alaska State Arts Council in Bethel, Skagway, and Hydaburg, Alaska in 1977.

Solo exhibitions

Panopticon Gallery, Boston, 1975 · M.I.T. Creative Photography Gallery, Cambridge, 1977 · Anchorage Historical and Fine Arts Museum; Alaska, 1977 · Southern Light, Amarillo, Texas, 1978 · Polaroid Gallery, Cambridge, 1978

Selected group exhibitions

Phoenix Art Museum, Arizona, 1969, 1970, 1971 · De-Cordova and Dana Museum, Lincoln, Massachusetts, 1972 · Wheaton College, Norton, Massachusetts, 1972 · Panopticon Gallery, Boston, 1972, 1973, 1976 · Fogg Art Museum, Cambridge, 1974, 1976 · Central Washington State College, Ellensburg, 1976 · Enjay Gallery, Boston, 1977

Collections

Fogg Art Museum; Polaroid Collection (Europa); private collections.

Mr. Stone's black-and-white photographs appear on pp. 60 through 63.

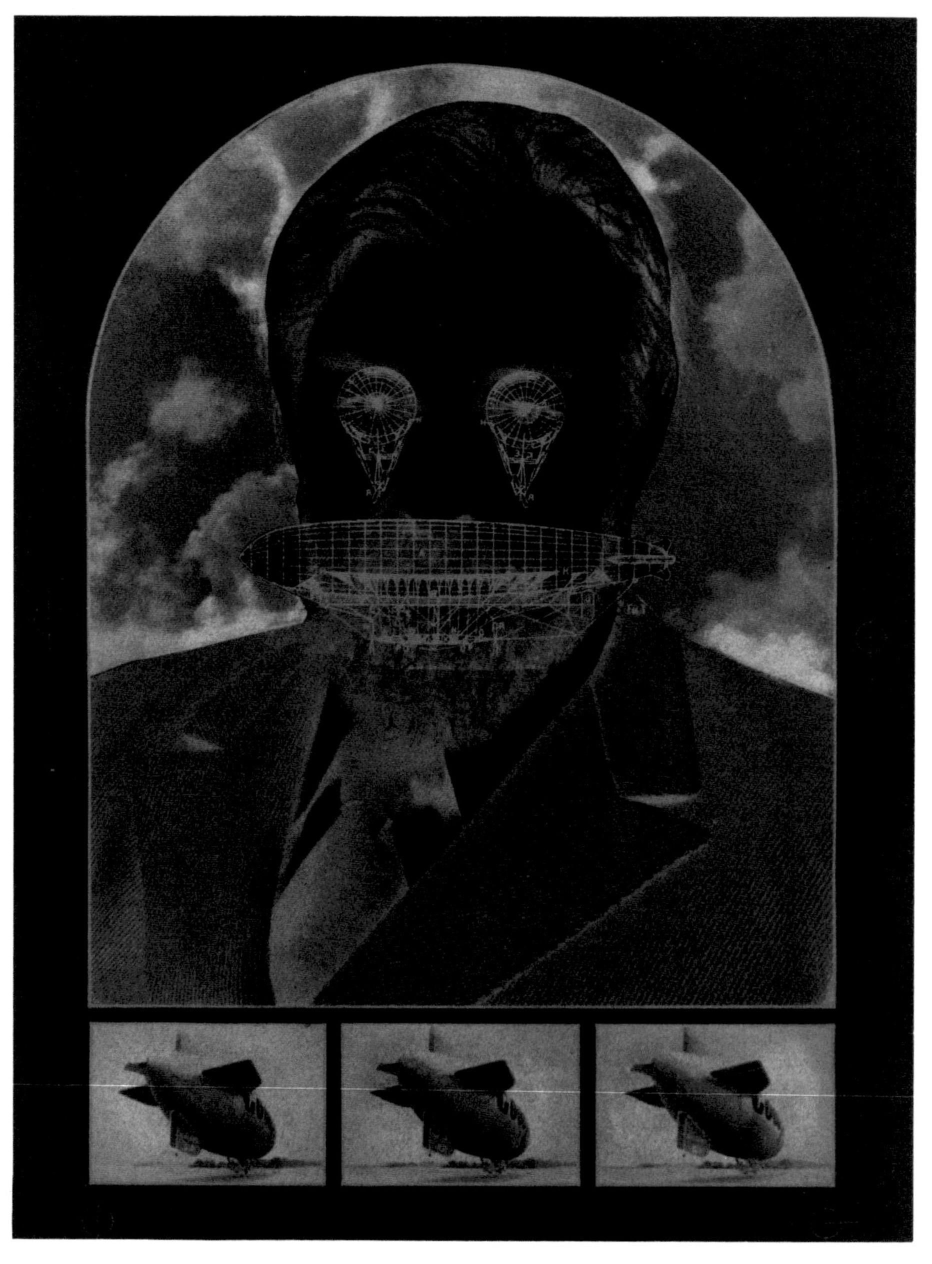

Ballooneer, 1974

STEPHEN ELSTON

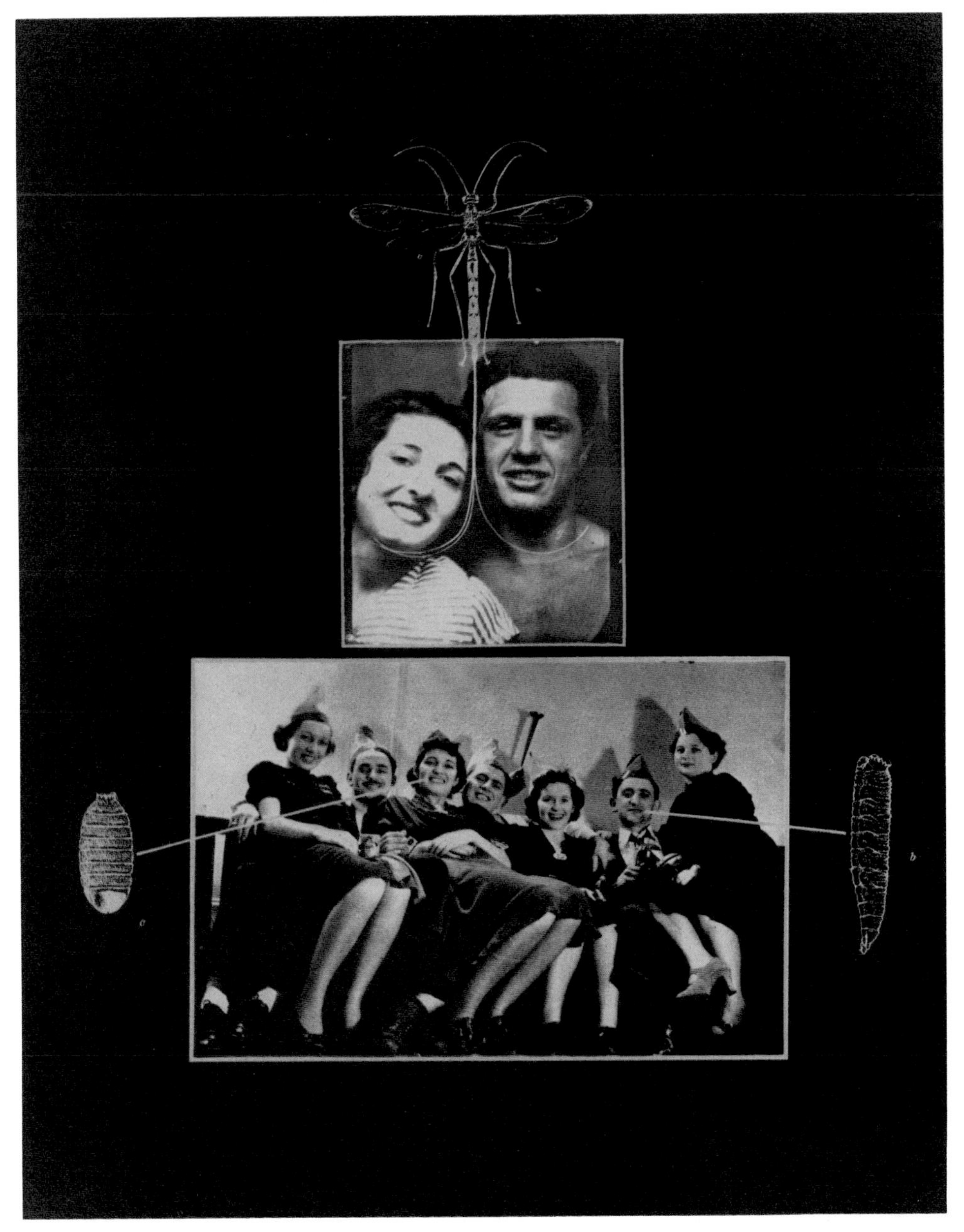

Faye and Ruby, 1974

STEPHEN ELSTON

41

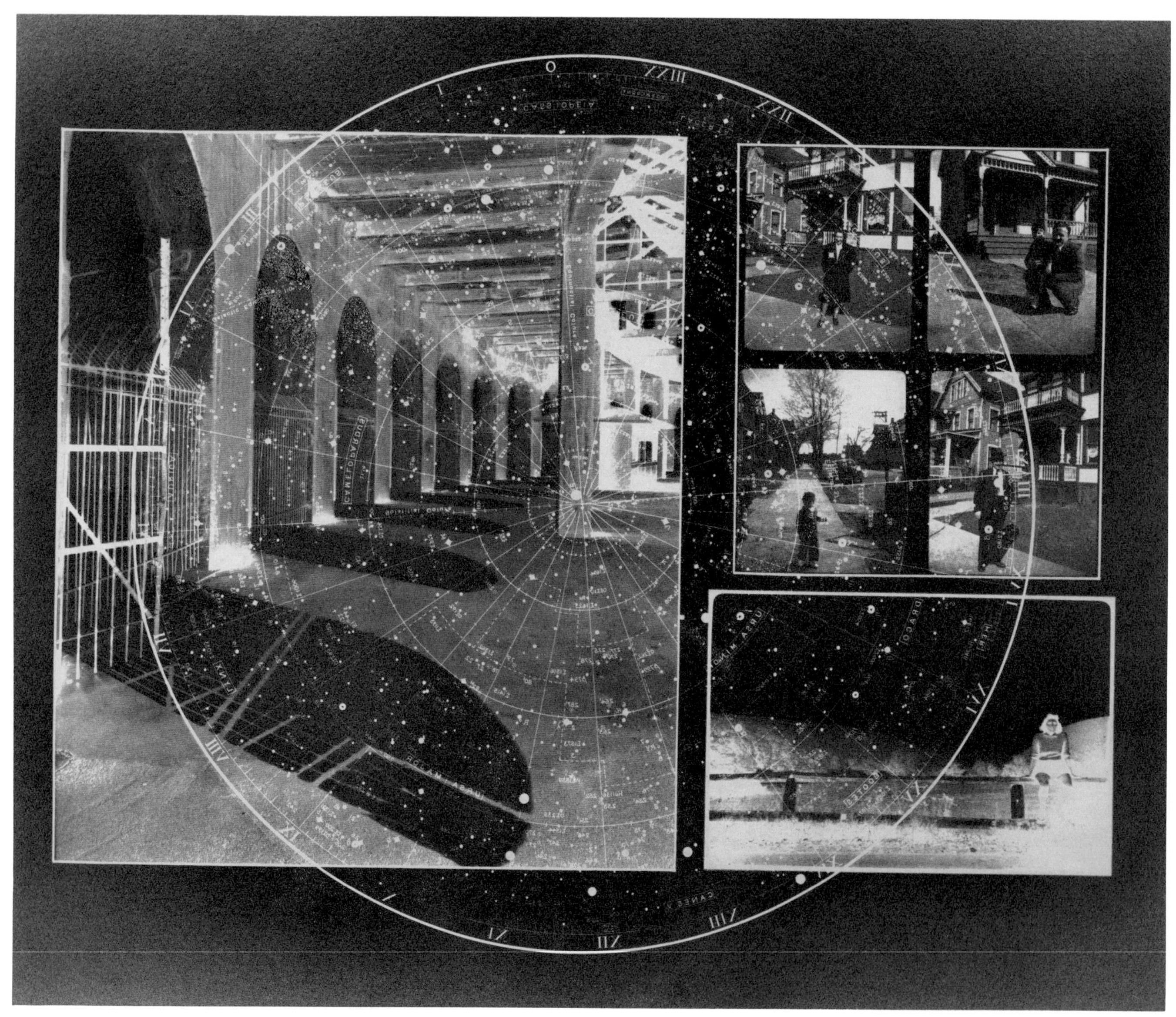

STEPHEN ELSTON · *Stargate, 1974*

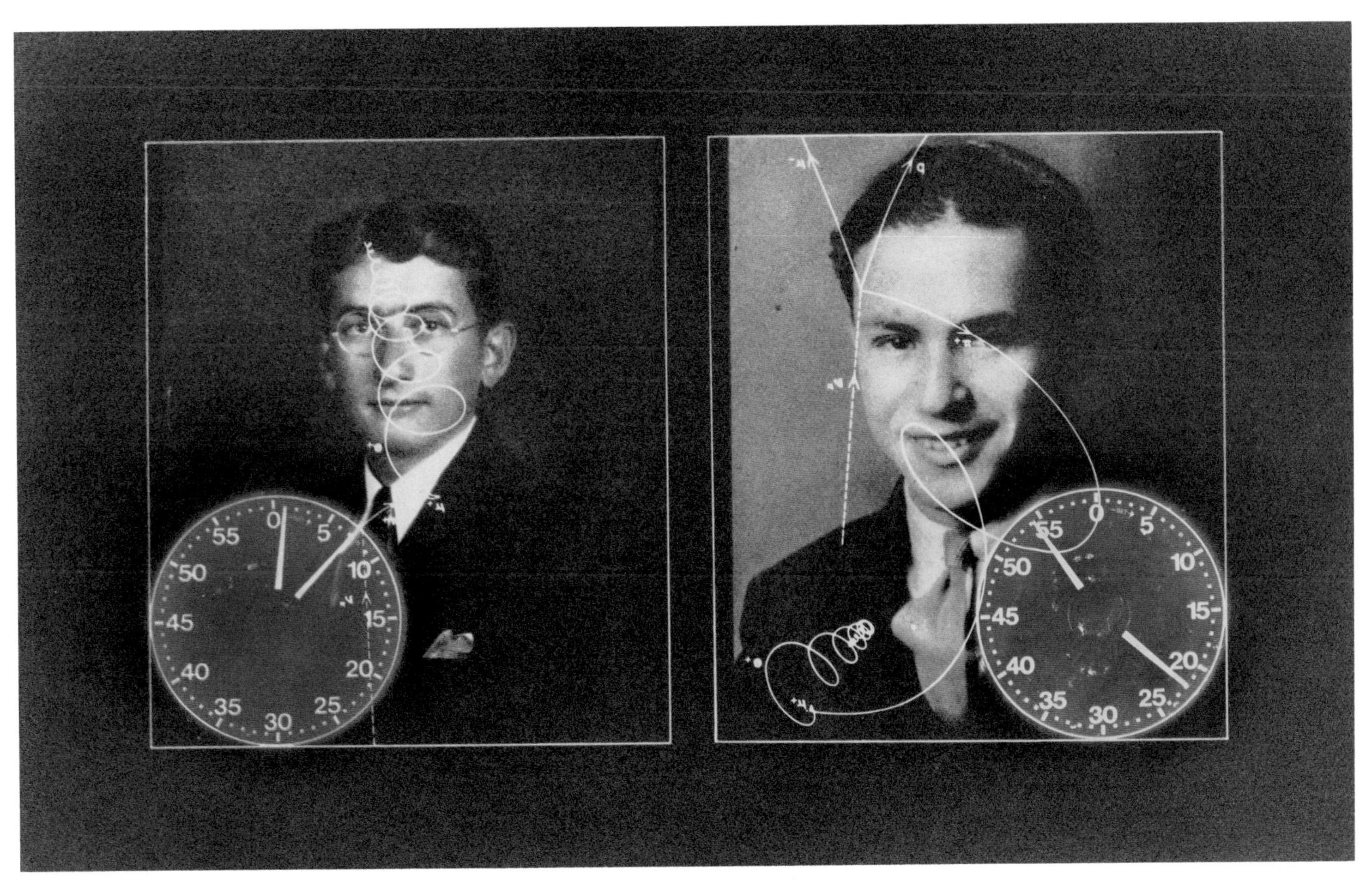

Archibald and Eddy, 1974 · STEPHEN ELSTON

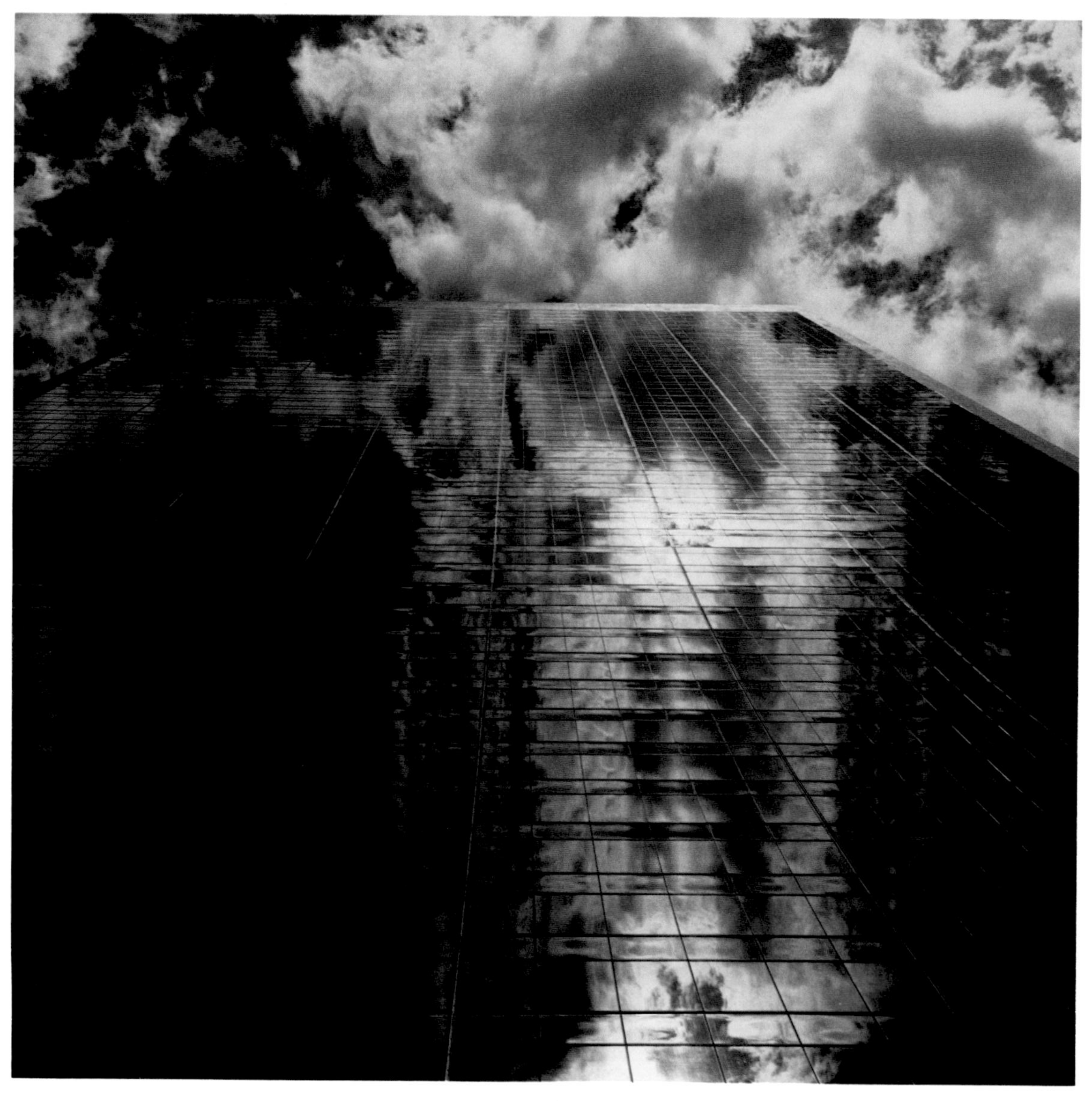

CHESTER MICHALIK · *New York, 1975*

44

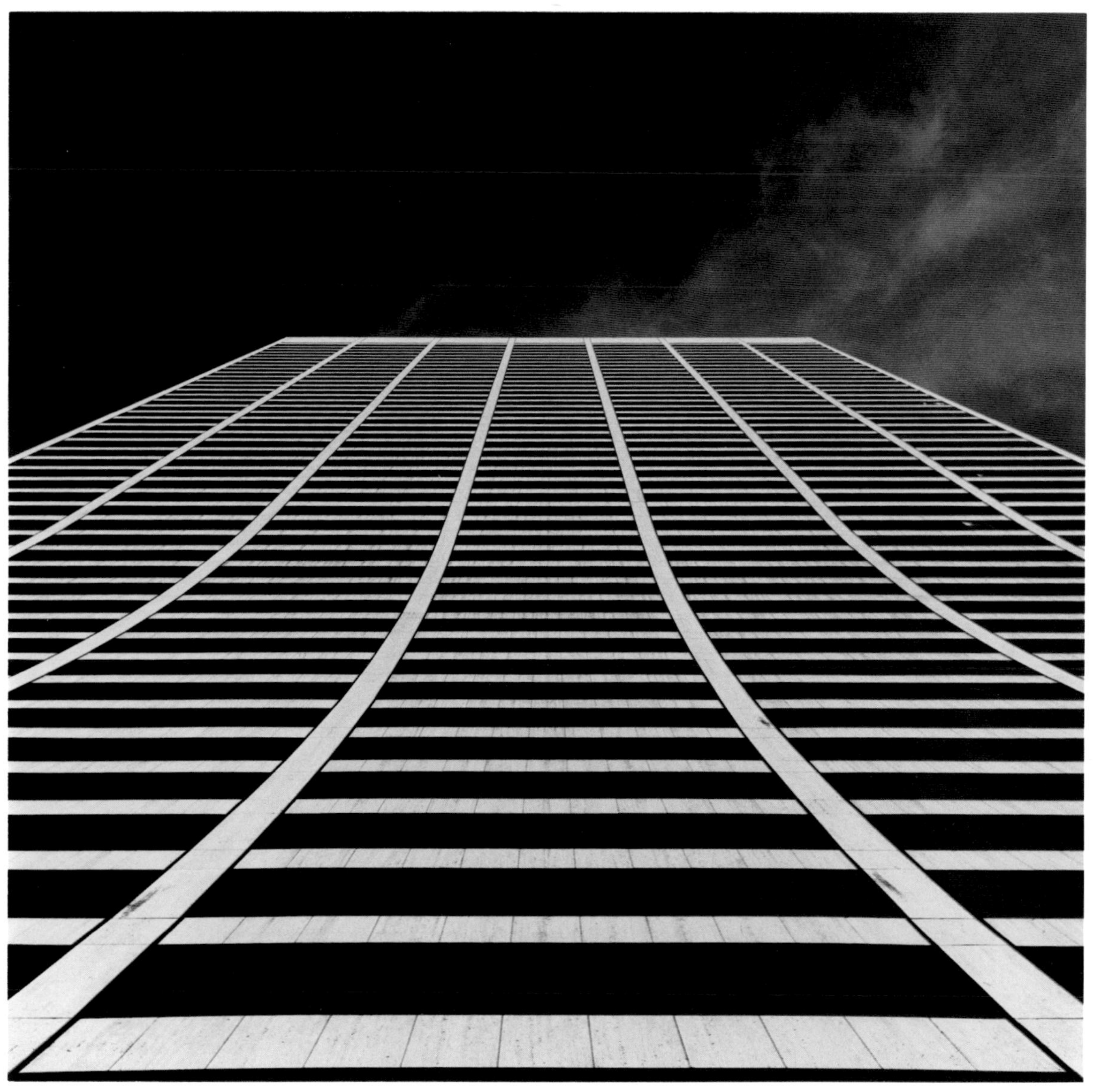

New York, 1975 · CHESTER MICHALIK

CHESTER MICHALIK · *DC-10, 1975*

Boston, Massachusetts, 1974 • CHESTER MICHALIK

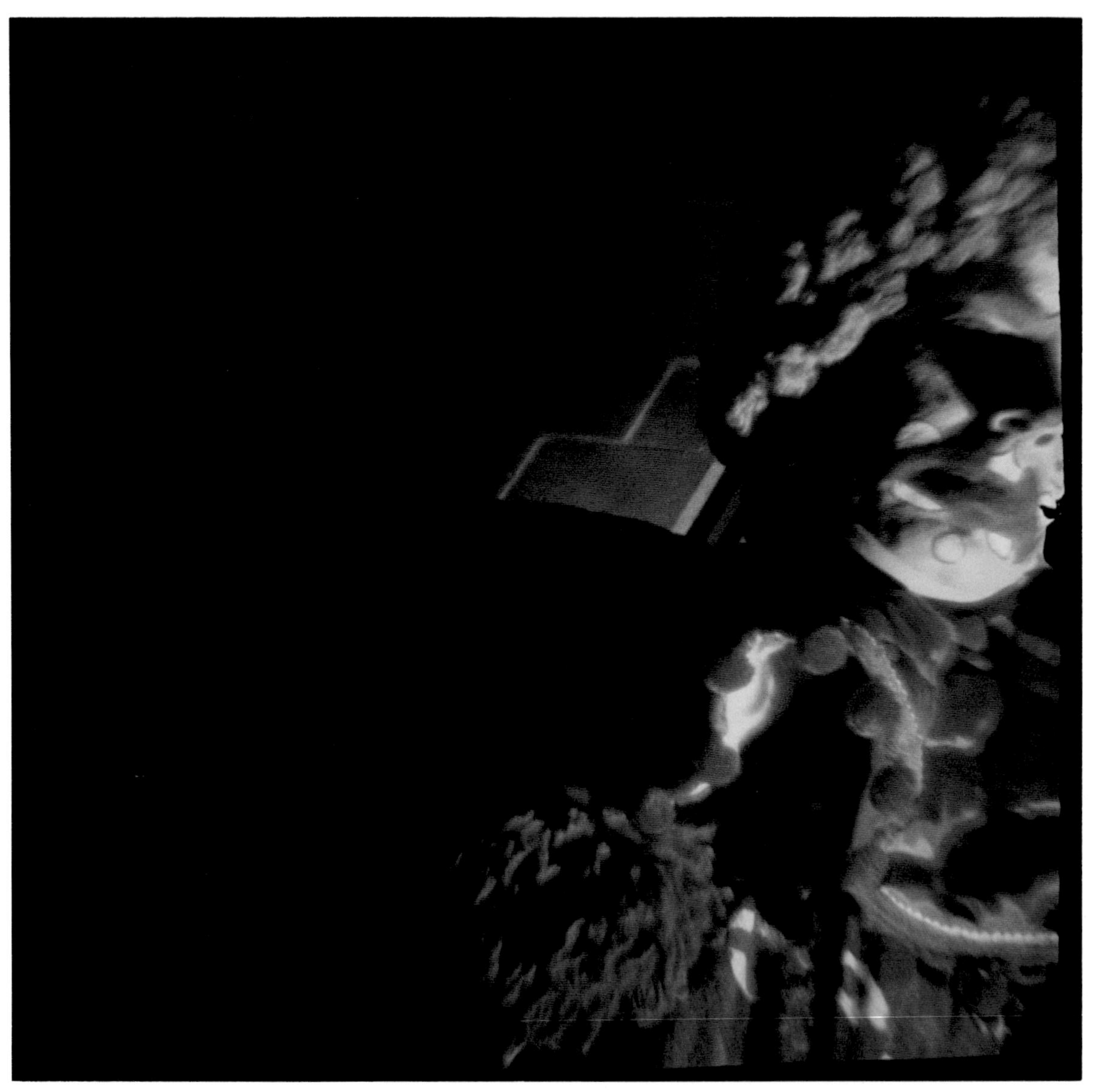

THOMAS PETIT · *1975*

48

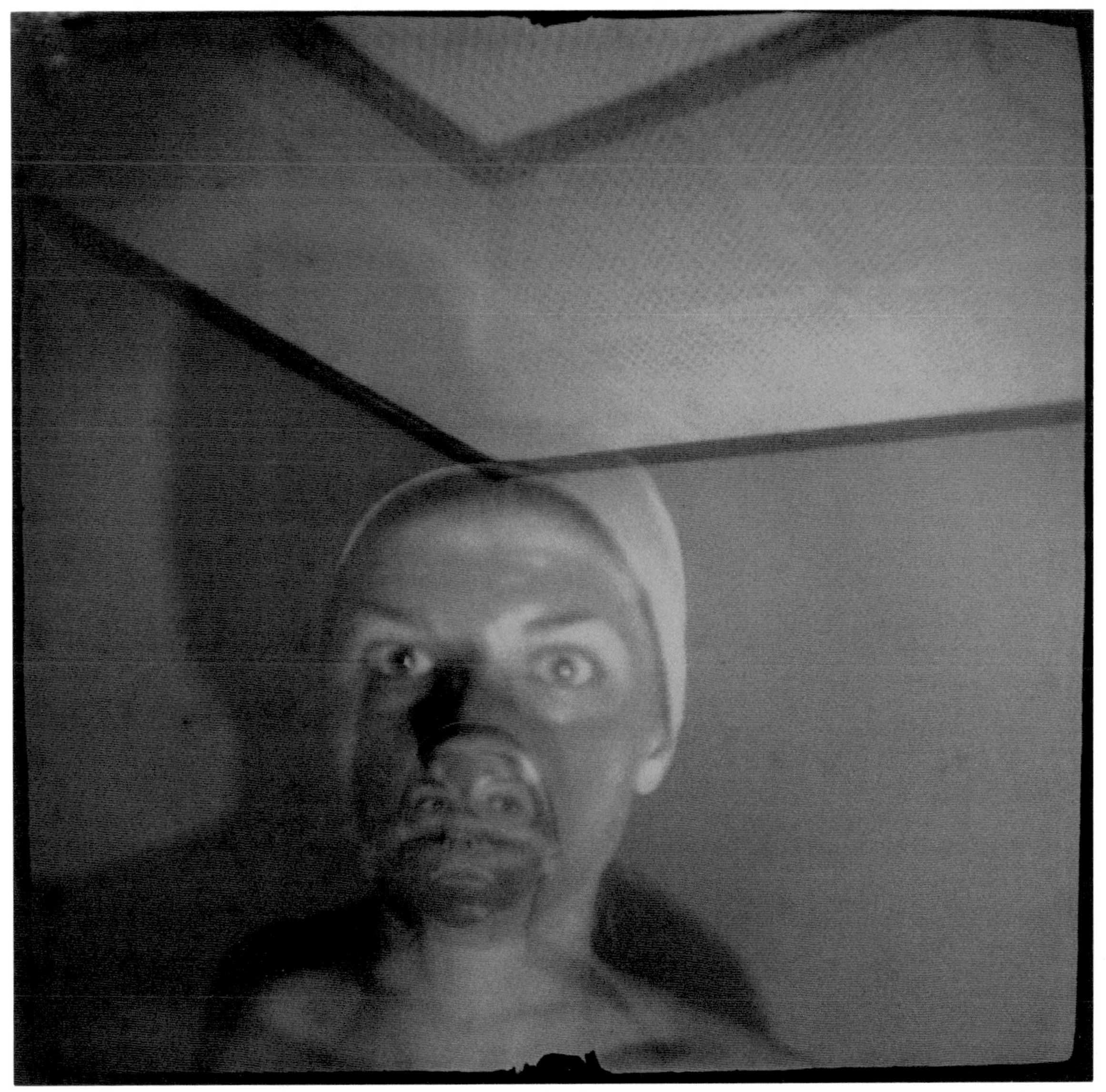

1977 · THOMAS PETIT

49

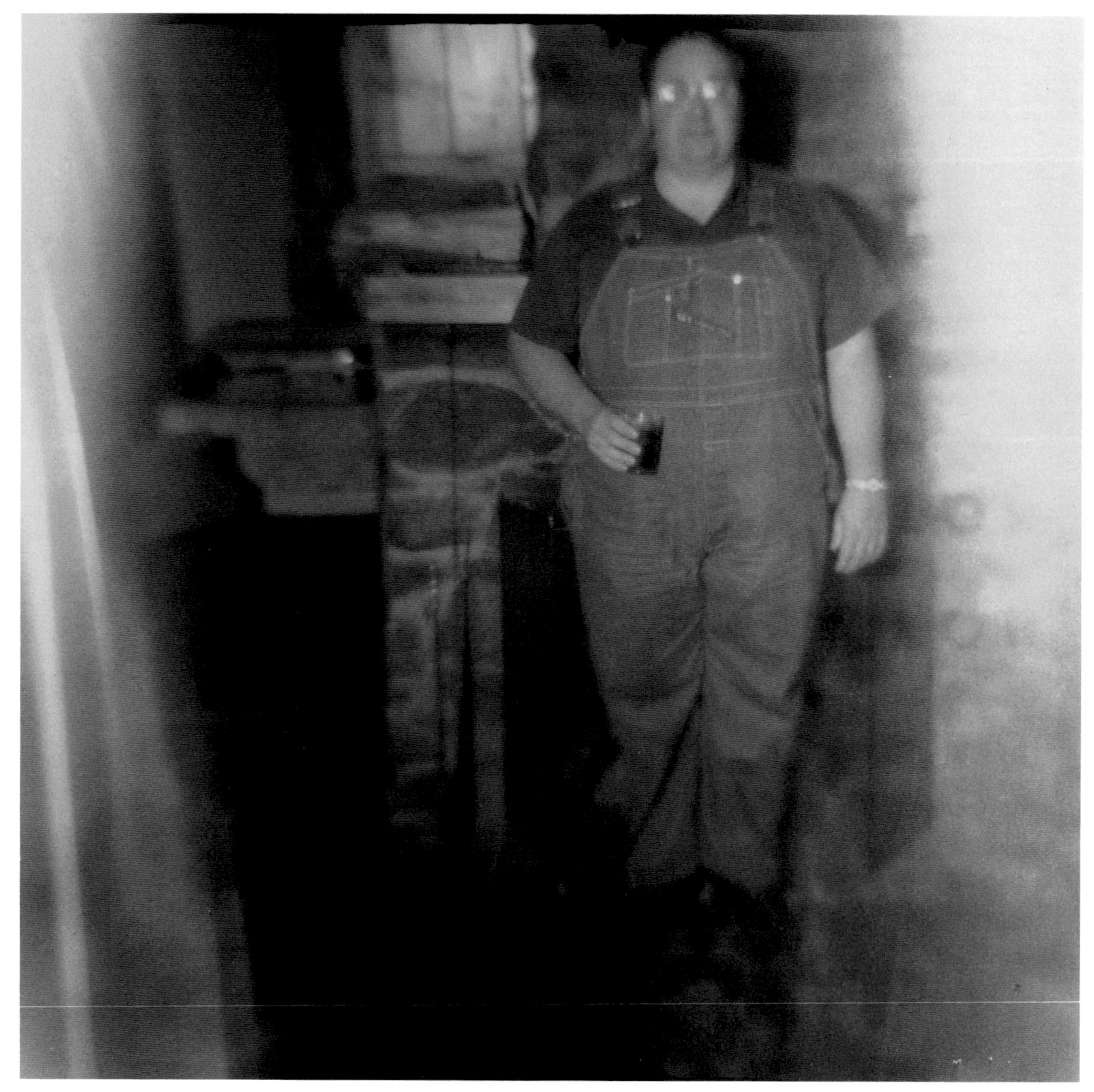

THOMAS PETIT · *1977*

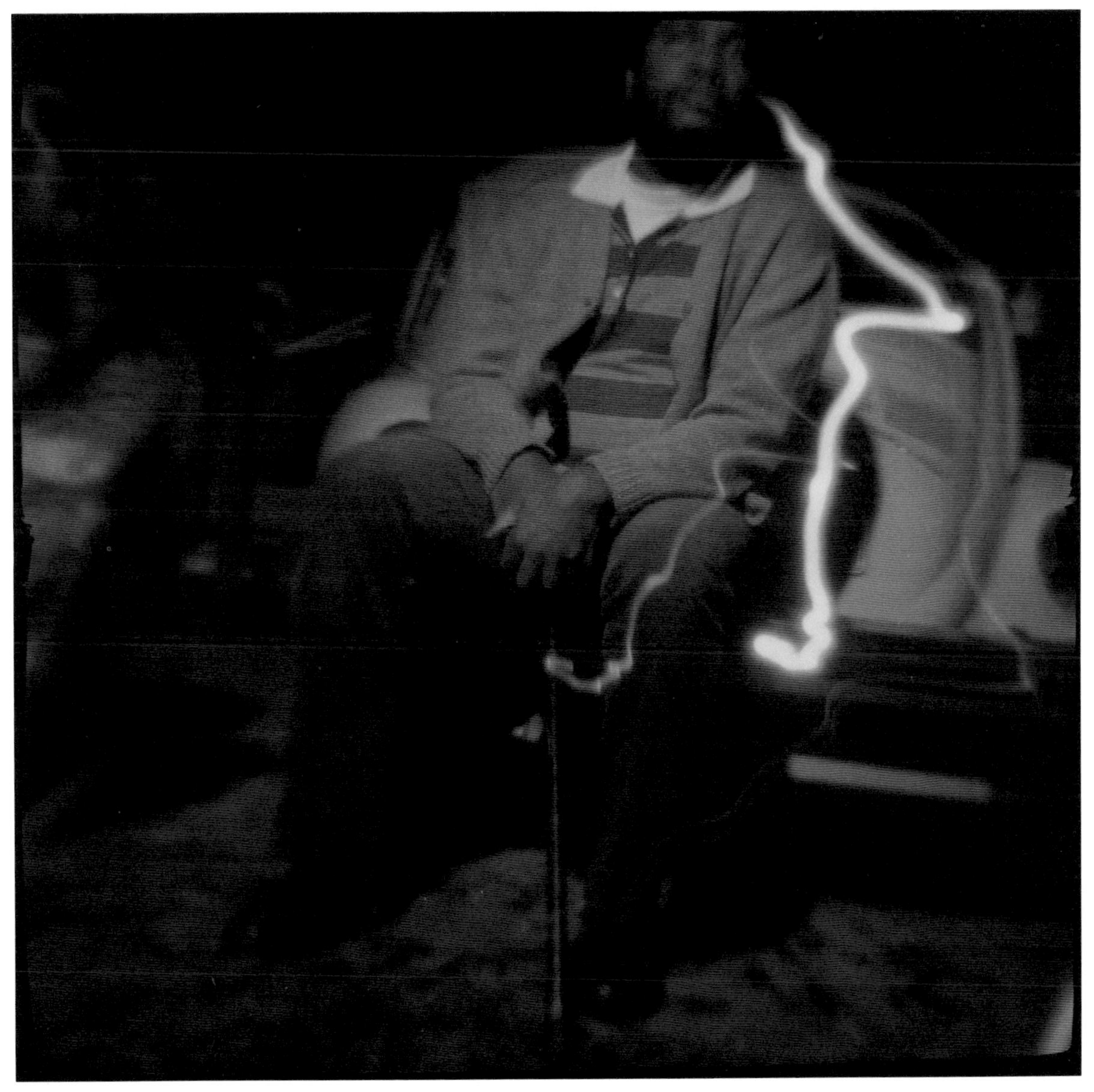

51

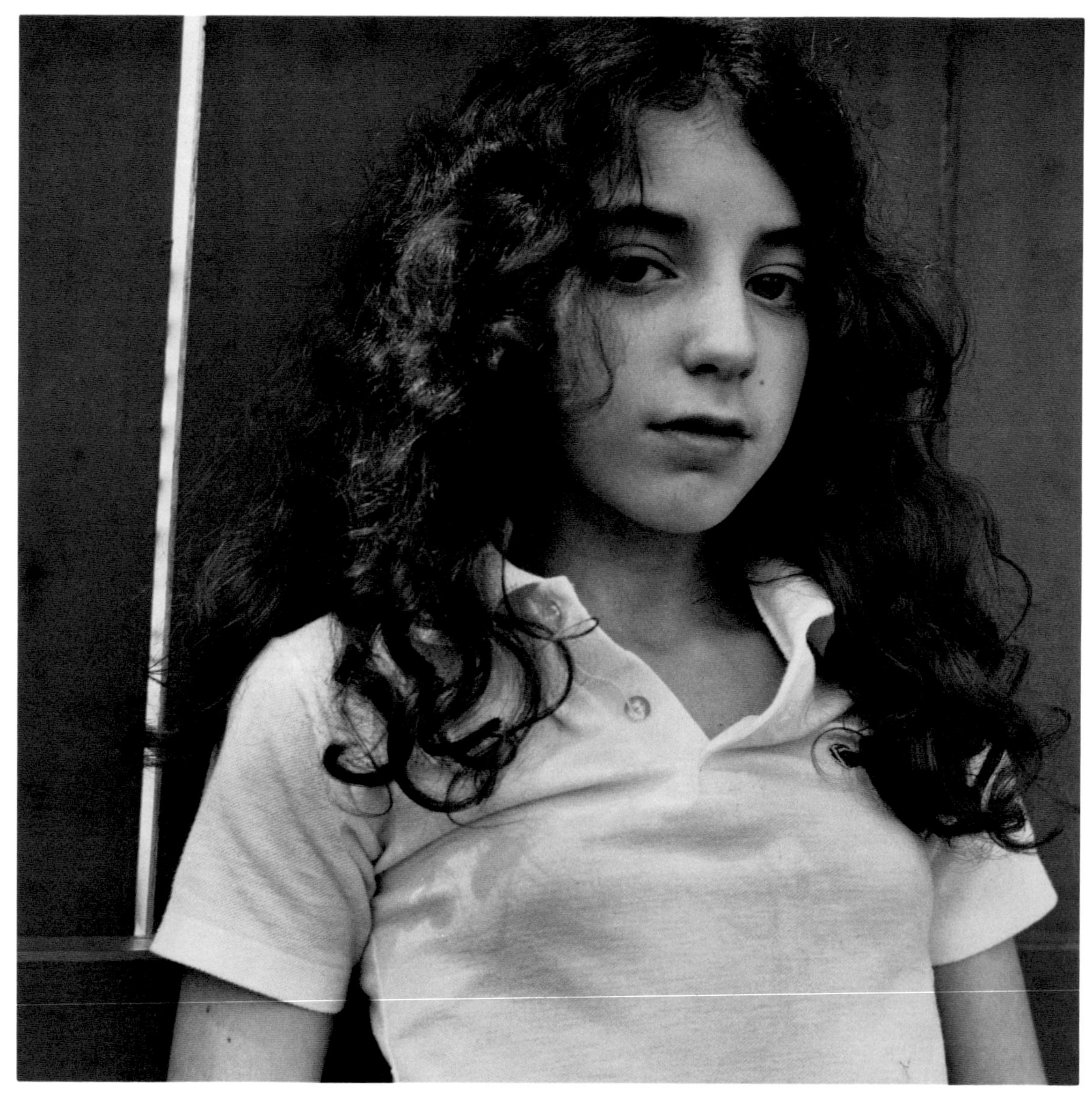

NANCY RANKIN · *Buffy, 7th Grade, 1974*

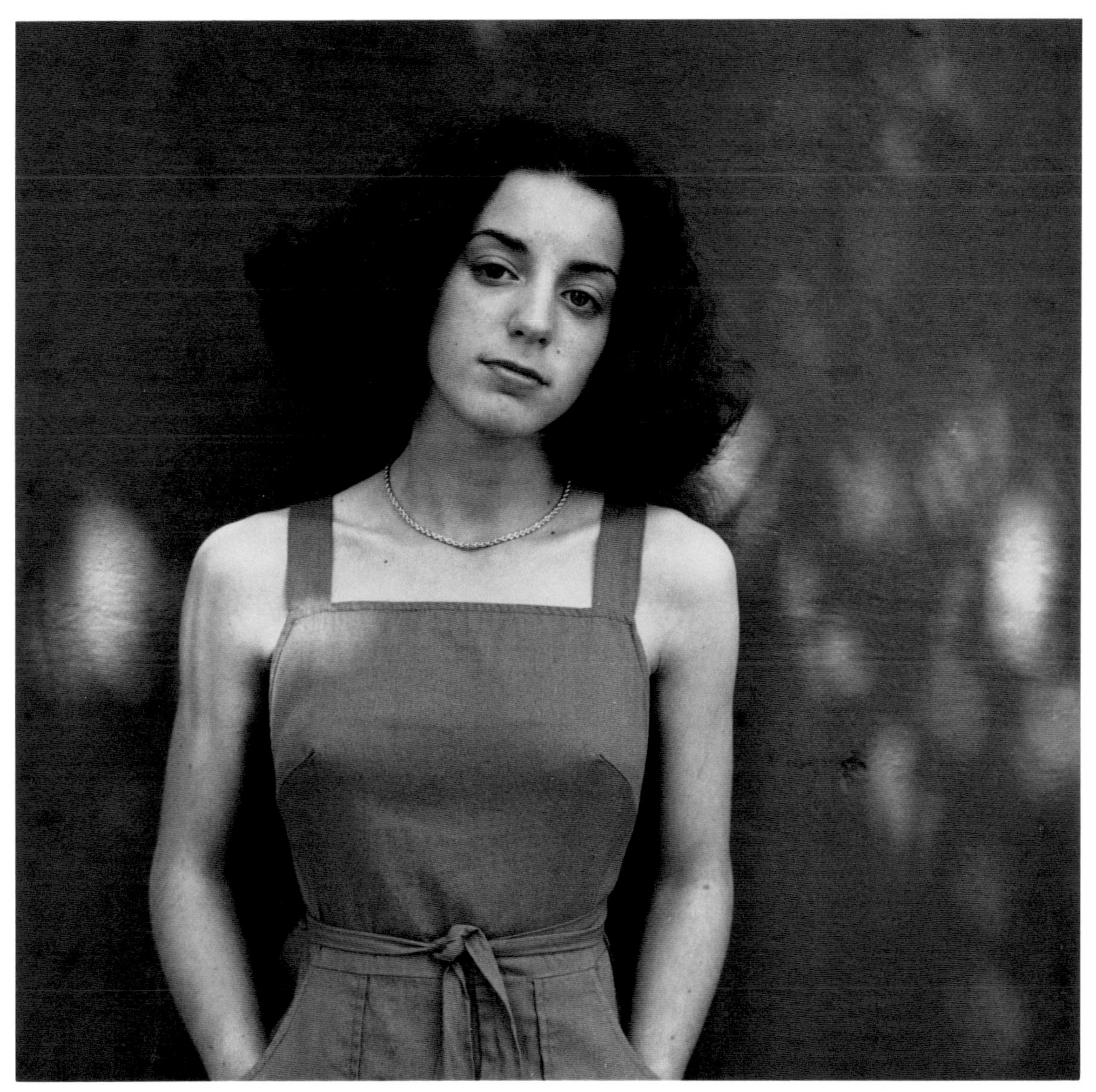

Buffy, 10th grade, 1977 · NANCY RANKIN

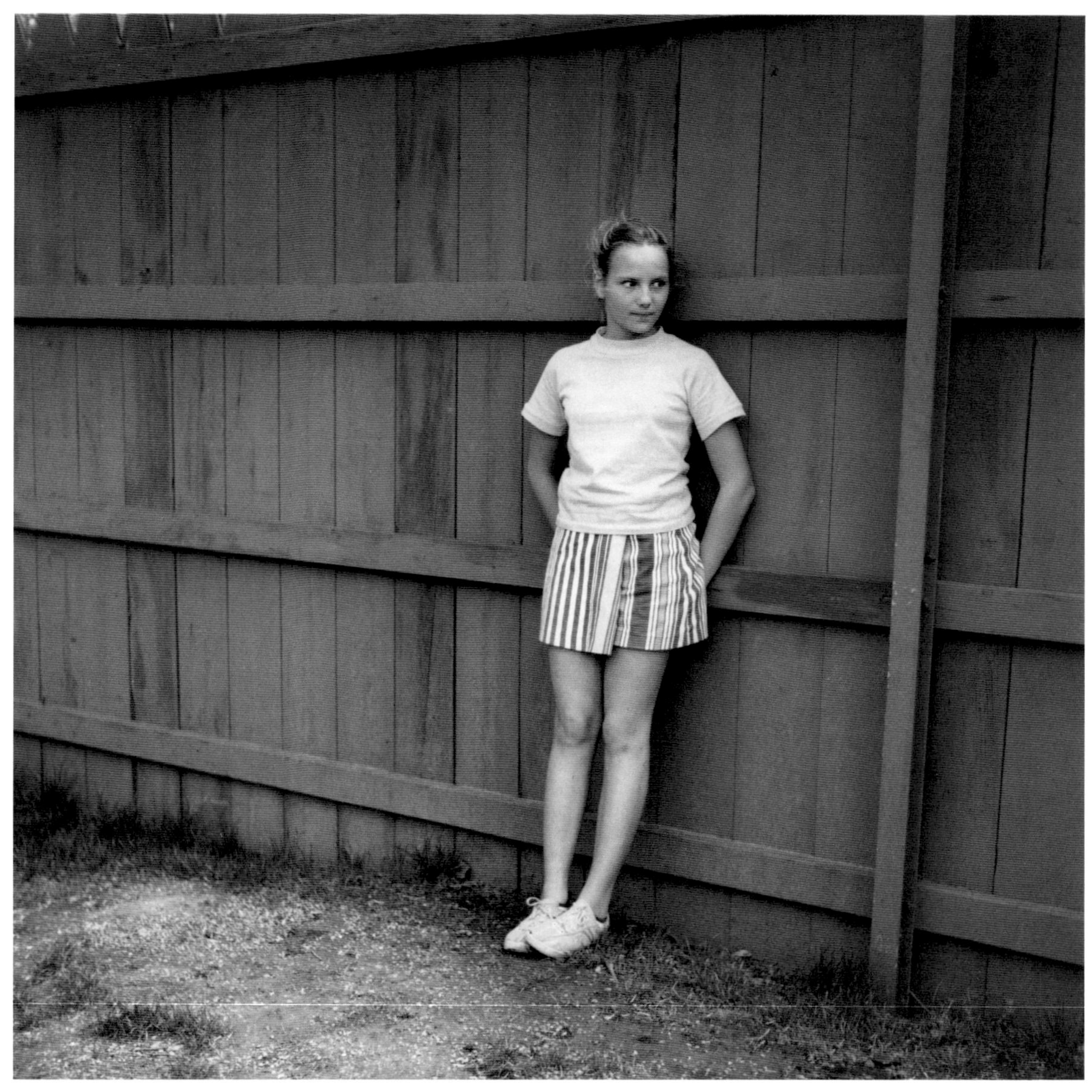

NANCY RANKIN · *Tina, 7th grade, 1974*

54

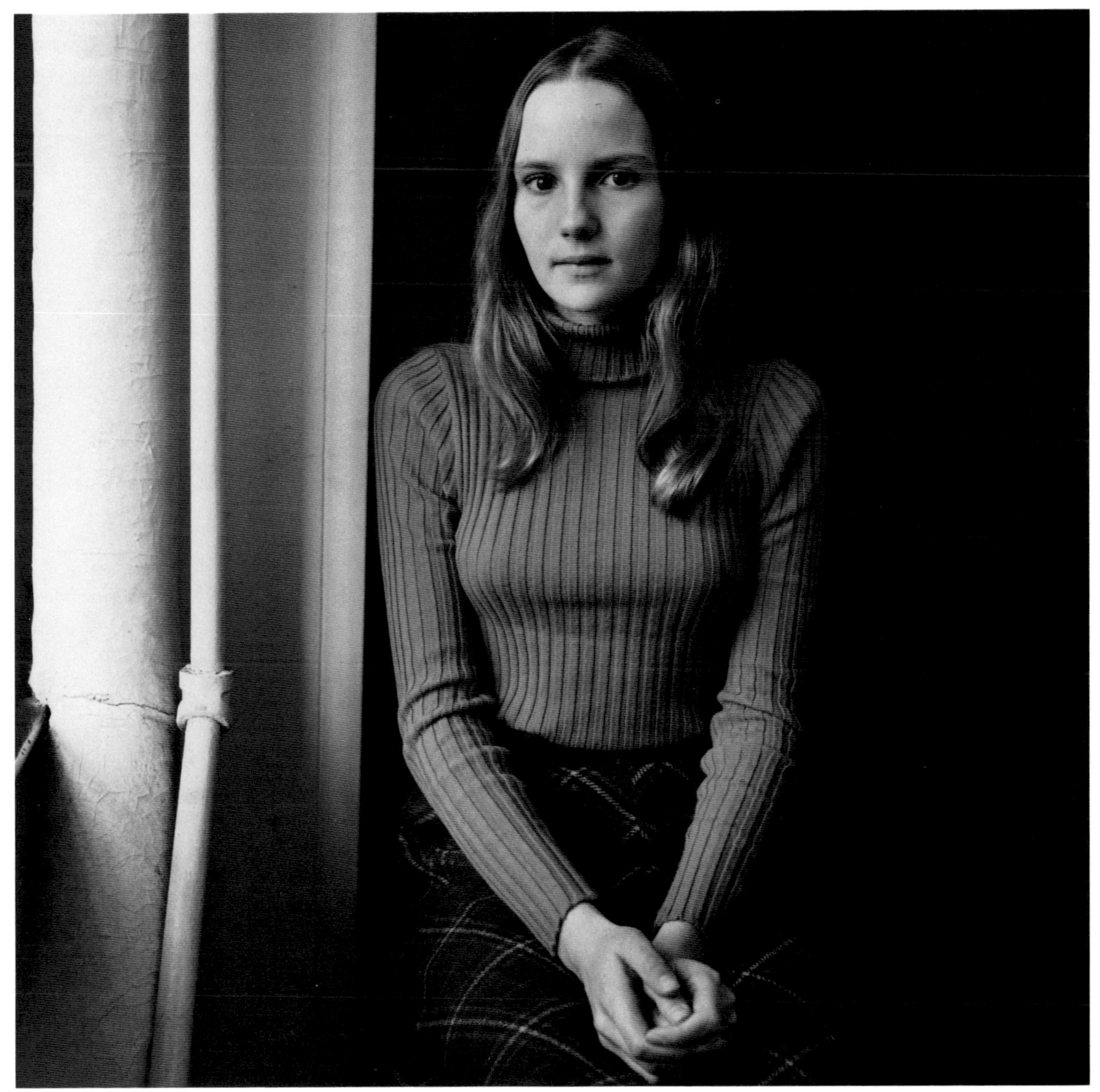

Tina, 9th grade, 1976 · NANCY RANKIN

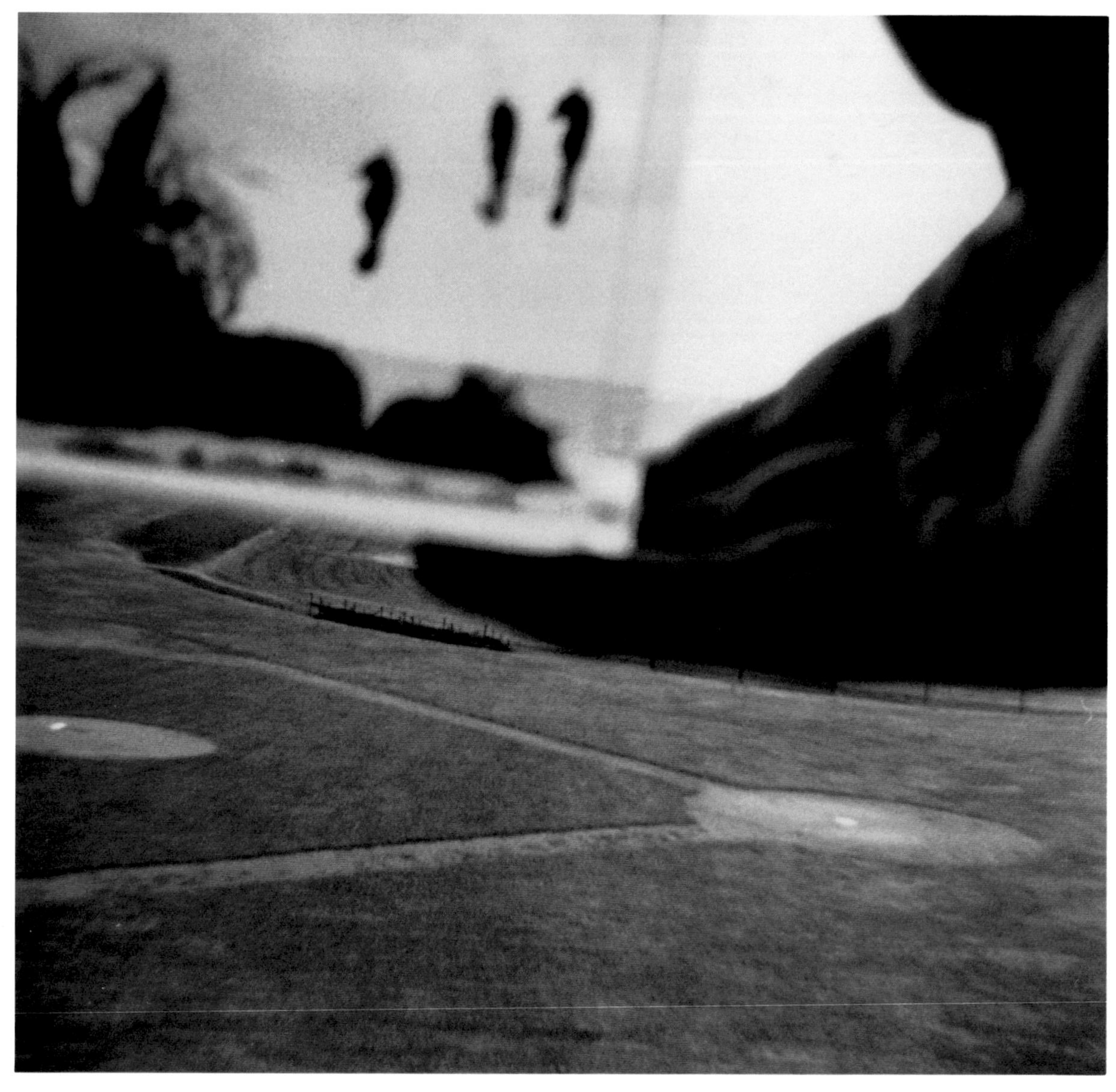

LAUREN SHAW · *Thompson's Island, Boston, Massachusetts, 1976*

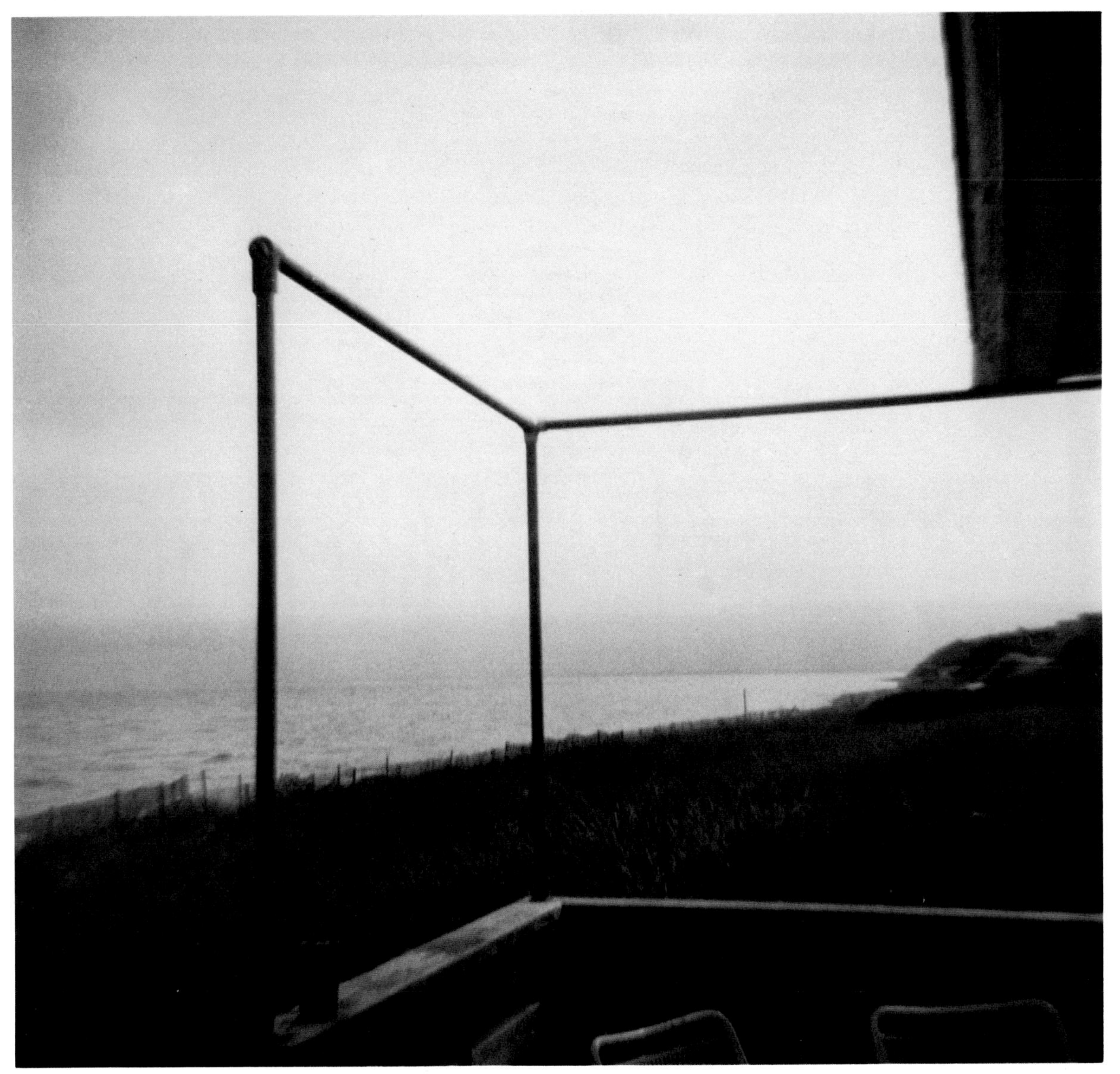

Cape Cod, Massachusetts, 1976 · LAUREN SHAW

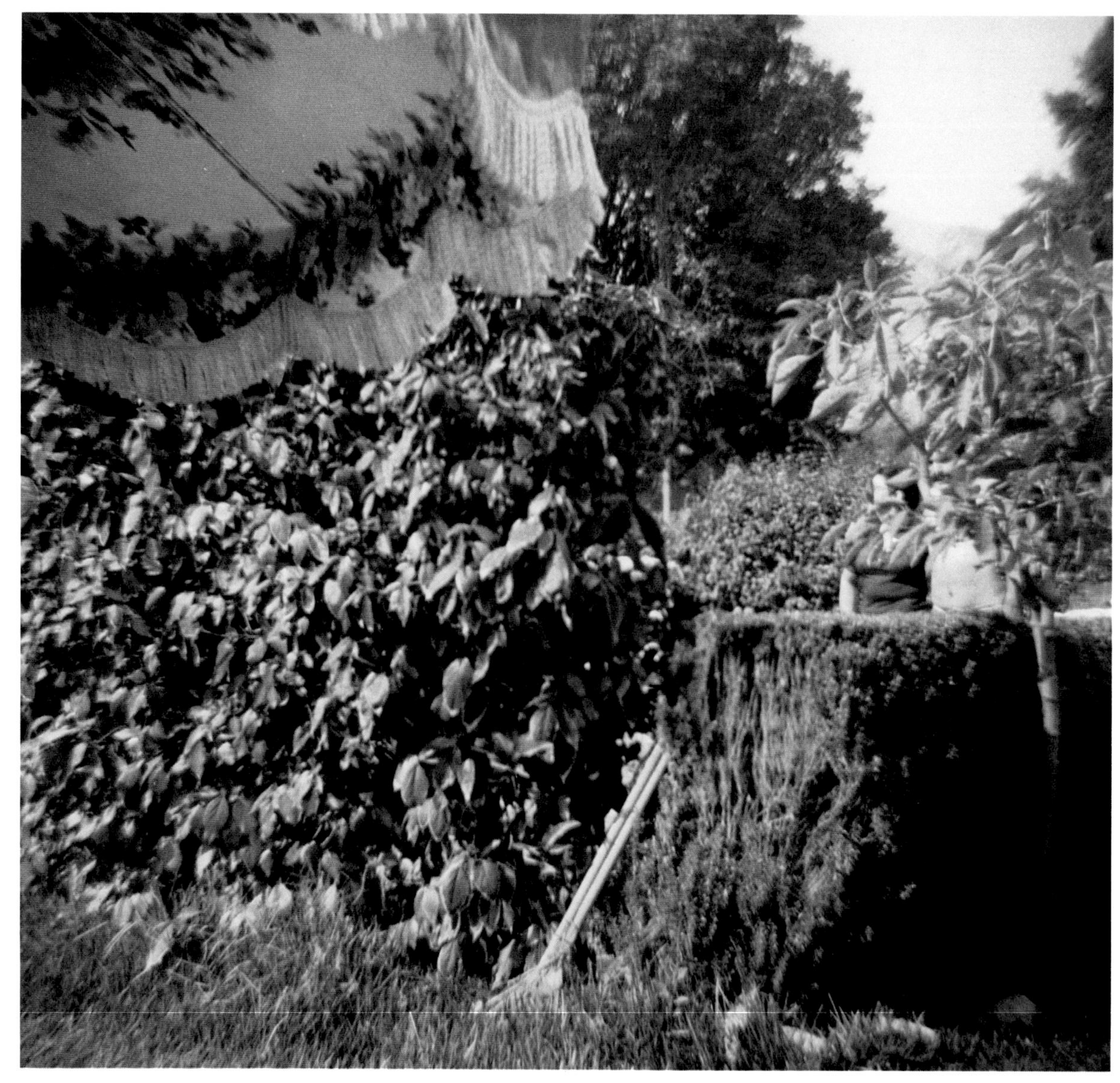

LAUREN SHAW · *Choisica, Peru, 1977*

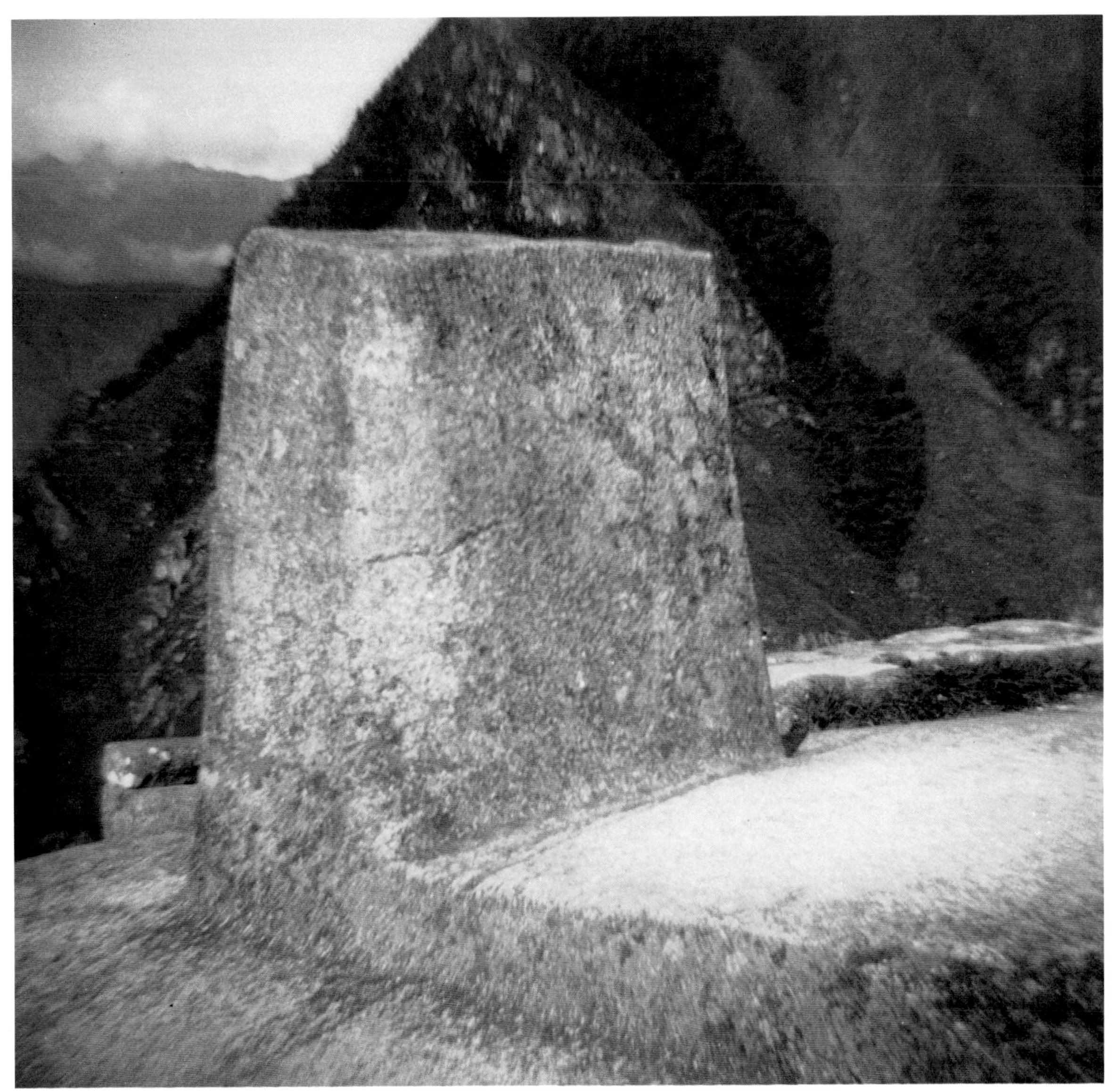

Machu Picchu, Peru, 1977 · LAUREN SHAW

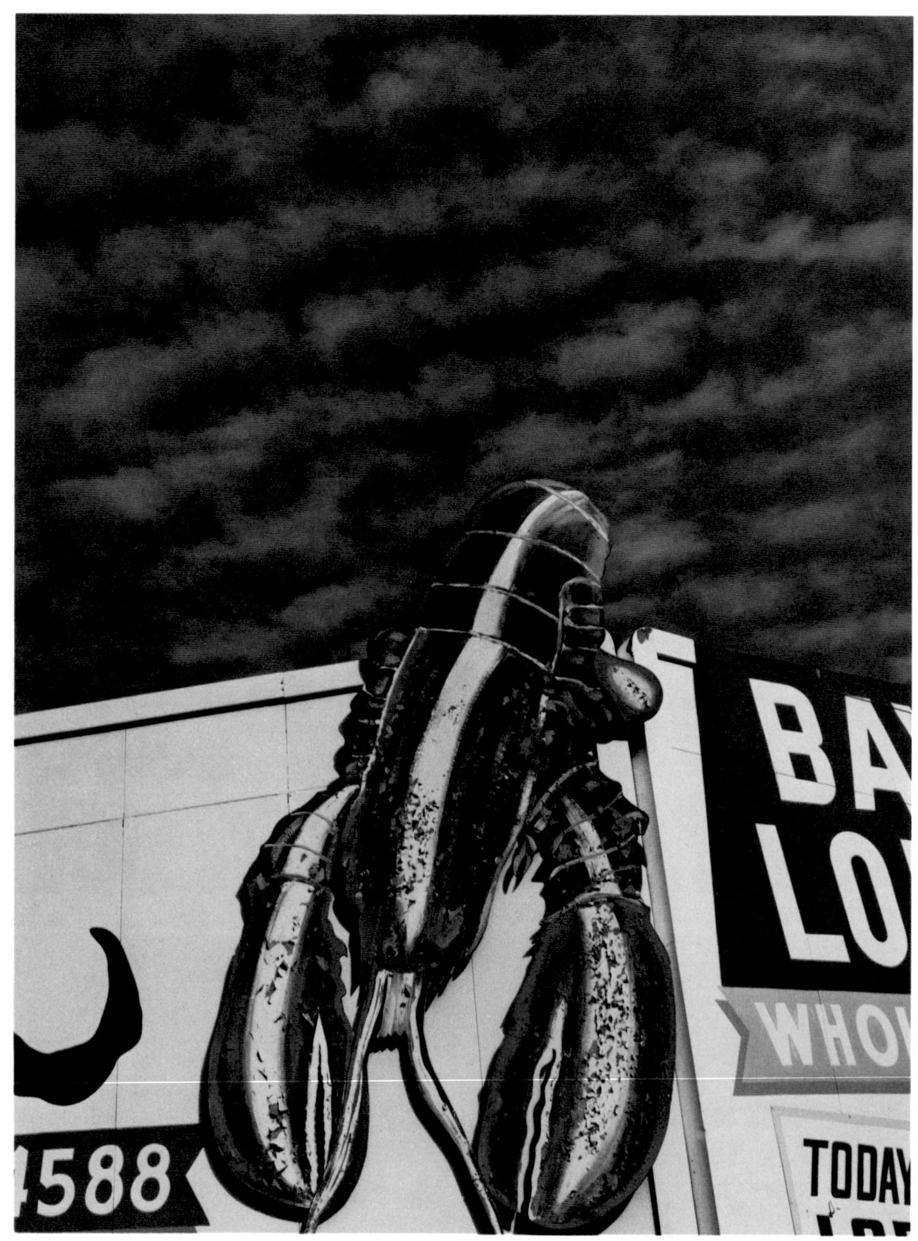

Boston, Massachusetts, 1975

JIM STONE

60

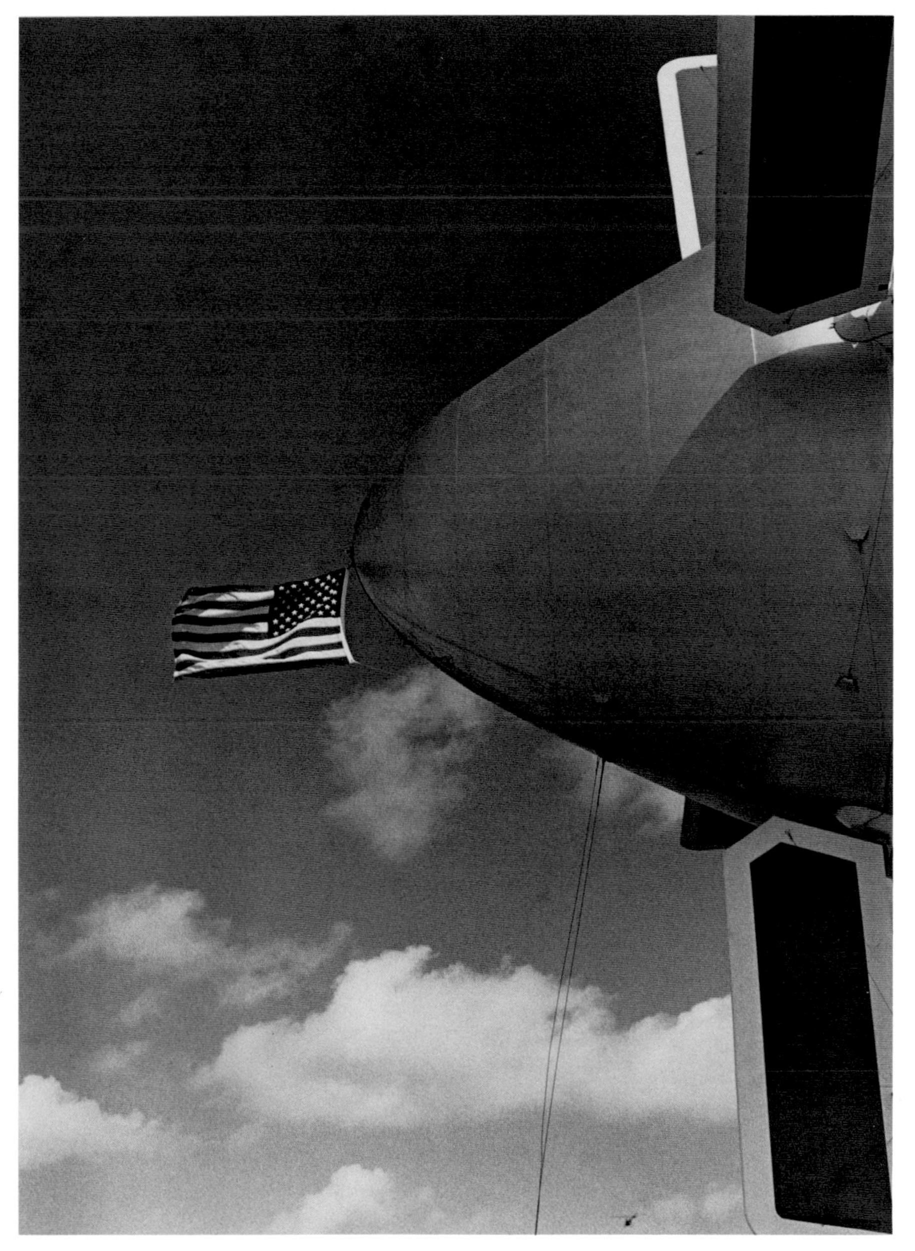

Miami, Florida, 1978

JIM STONE

61

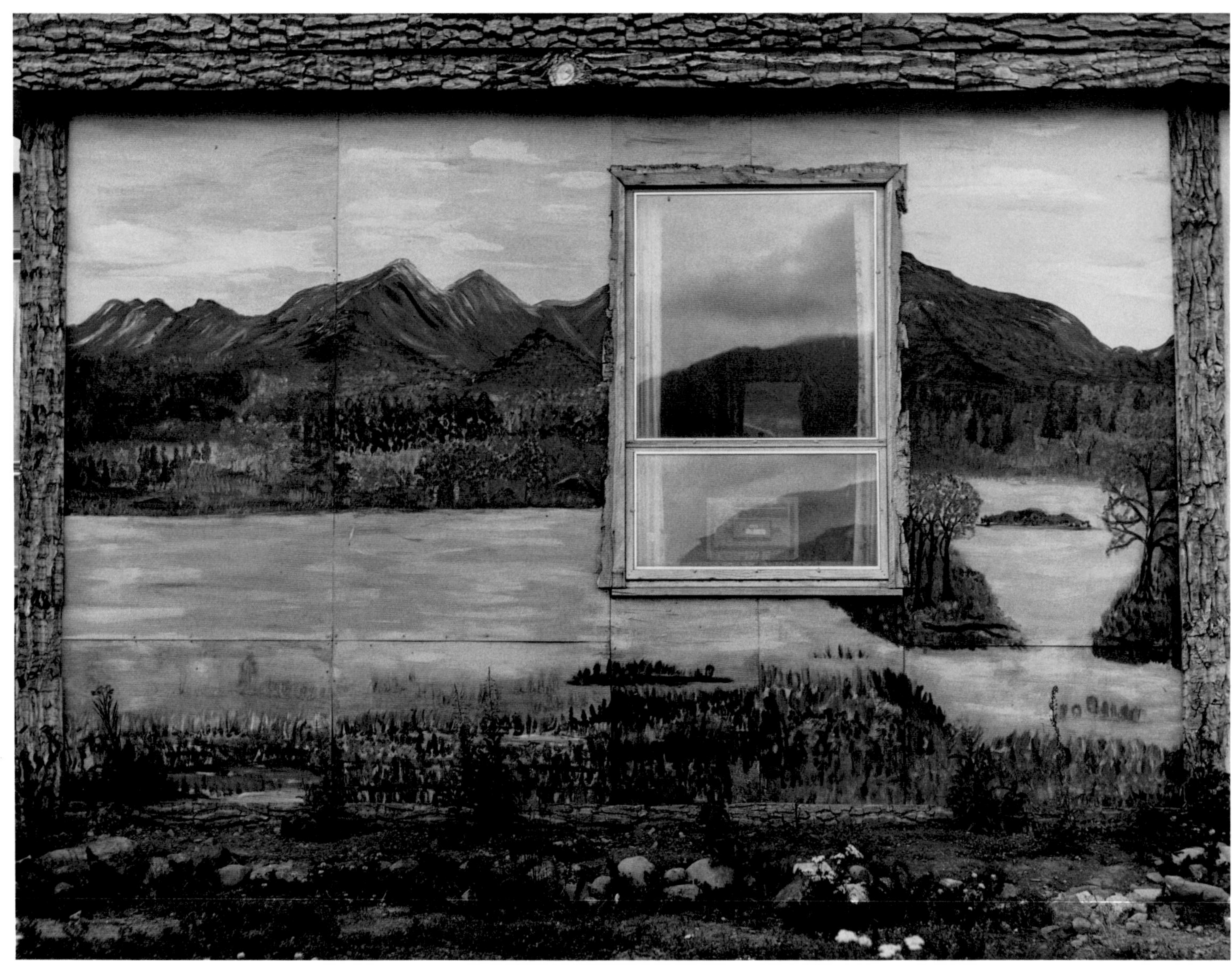

JIM STONE · *Indian, Alaska, 1975*

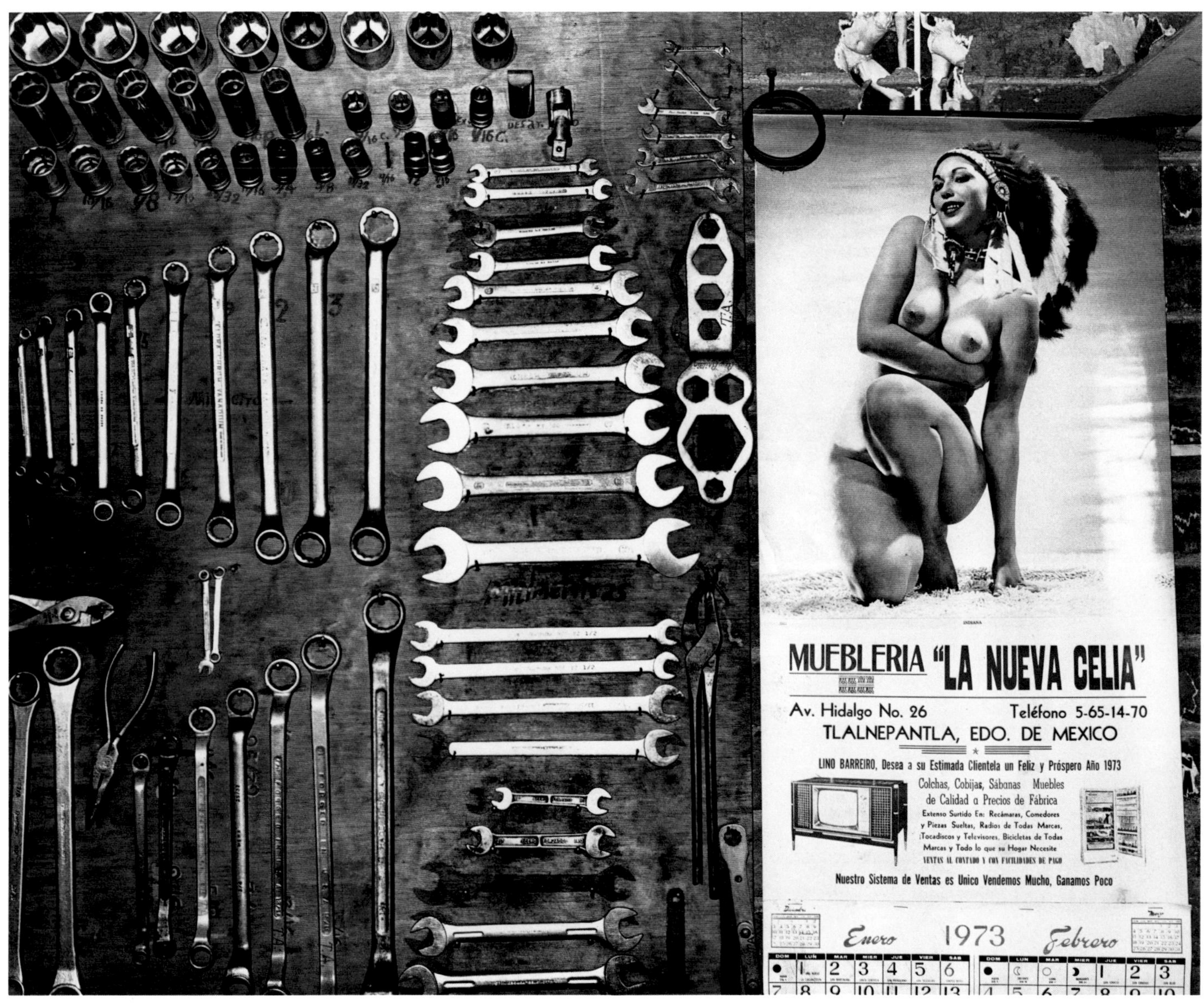

Mexico City, 1974 · JIM STONE

63

1977 Fellowship Recipients

Biographies

The panelists were BERENICE ABBOTT, JOAN LYONS and RAY METZKER. The seven recipients were selected from 485 applicants.

KEN BROWN, *Cambridge*

Born 1944, Dayton, Ohio
Education: University of Massachusetts; Boston University

Ken Brown is a free-lance photographer, filmmaker and cartoonist. He is currently a consultant for the Cambridge Arts Council and the author of a series of photographic postcards and posters. He has taught filmmaking in several Boston suburban public schools and is currently teaching animation at Boston College.

Solo exhibition

Prospect Street Photo Gallery, Cambridge, 1976

Group exhibitions

Mules Mirage Gallery, Cambridge, 1977 · M.I.T. Creative Photography Gallery, Cambridge, 1978

Publications

Saturday Review; Ginn & Co. children's textbooks; *Dark Horse,* fiction and photography journal (co-editor)

Mr. Brown's black-and-white photographs appear on pp. 68 through 71.

RUTH GREEN, *Greenfield*

Born 1949, Indianapolis, Indiana
Education: Wellesley College; Yale University, B.A.

Ruth Green is a free-lance writer and photographer. The photographs reproduced in this book are from a series of street portraits taken in New Haven, Connecticut.

Group exhibitions

Stratton Arts Festival, Vermont, 1973; M.I.T. Creative Photography Gallery, Cambridge, 1978.

Ms. Green's black-and-white photographs appear on pp. 72 through 75.

BRUCE KINCH, *Somerville*

Born 1944, Yonkers, New York
Education: Tufts University, B.S.; California Institute of

the Arts, M.F.A.; studied photography with Ben Lifson
and Minor White.

Bruce Kinch served as a photographic specialist for the
Polaroid Corporation from 1966 to 1970. He is currently
Assistant Chairman of the Photography Department at the
Art Institute of Boston. He has taught at Harvard University, Cambridge, Emerson College, Boston, and Imageworks, Cambridge.

Solo exhibitions

Polaroid Corporation, Cambridge, 1970 · Garland Junior
College, Boston, 1973 · Harvard University, 1974

Group exhibitions

M.I.T., Cambridge, 1967, 1970 · Boston Visual Artists
Union, 1975 · M.I.T. Creative Photography Gallery, 1978

Mr. Kinch's black-and-white photographs appear on pp. 76
through 79.

KIPTON KUMLER, *Lexington*

Born 1940, Cleveland, Ohio
Education: Cornell University, bachelor's degree; Cornell

and Harvard Universities, master's degrees.

Kipton Kumler is a free-lance photographer who teaches
large-format photography privately. He works with a consulting firm in Cambridge, Massachusetts.

Solo exhibitions

Polaroid Gallery, Cambridge, 1972 · M.I.T. Creative Photography Gallery, Cambridge, 1974 · Carl Siembab Gallery,
Boston, 1974 · Robert Schoelkopf Gallery, New York
City, 1975 · Douglas Kenyon Gallery, Chicago, 1976 ·
Cronin Gallery, Houston, Texas, 1977 · Grapestake Gallery, San Francisco, 1978

Group exhibitions

Institute of Contemporary Art, Boston, 1972 · Museum of
Fine Arts, Boston, 1975 · Addison Gallery of American Art,
Andover, Massachusetts, 1974 (two-person) · Galeria da
Emenda, Lisbon, Portugal, 1975 · Vision Gallery, Boston,
1976 · G. Ray Hawkins Gallery, Los Angeles, 1977 (two-person) · Jewett Arts Center, Wellesley College, Massachusetts, 1977 · University of New Hampshire, Durham, 1977
· M.I.T. Creative Photography Gallery, 1978

Publications

Camera, 1970; *Fox,* 1972; *British Journal of Photography,*

1973; *Popular Photography*, 1975; *Kipton Kumler, Photographs*, 1975, David R. Godine, publisher; *A Portfolio of Plants, Ten Platinum and Palladium Prints*, ed. 50, 1977.

Selected collections

Museum of Fine Arts, Boston; Bibliothèque Nationale, Paris; Addison Gallery of American Art; Worcester Art Museum, Massachusetts; Metropolitan Museum of Art, New York City; Johnson Museum at Cornell University, Ithaca, New York; George Eastman House, Rochester, New York; University of Nebraska, Lincoln; Columbus Art Museum, Ohio.

Mr. Kumler's black-and-white photographs appear on pp. 80 through 83.

KEVIN MONAGHAN, *Westwood*

Born 1948, Dorchester, Massachusetts
Education: B.F.A., Boston, Massachusetts

Kevin Monaghan has taught photography in several colleges and private schools in the New England area and is presently teaching at Bridgewater State College, Bridgewater, Massachusetts. He is also a free-lance photographer.

Solo exhibitions

Thorne Art Gallery, Keene State College, New Hampshire, 1975 · Kohler Arts Center, Sheboygan, Wisconsin, 1976

Group exhibitions

Zone V Gallery, Watertown, Massachusetts, 1971 · M.I.T. Creative Photography Gallery, Cambridge, 1978

Publications

Young American Photography, vol. 1.

Mr. Monaghan's black-and-white photographs appear on pp. 84 through 87.

JONATHAN MORSE, *Cambridge*

Born 1948, New York City
Education: Yale University, B.A.; State University of New York (Visual Studies Workshop), M.F.A.

Jonathan Morse is a color photographer and printmaker who has taught various workshops at Smith College, Northampton, Massachusetts, Haystack Mountain School of Crafts, Maine, and the Visual Studies Workshop,

Rochester. He is currently attending Boston College Law School.

Solo exhibition

Tyler School of Art, Philadelphia, 1977

Selected group exhibitions

Addison Gallery of American Art, Andover, Massachusetts, 1975 · Ohio State University, Columbus, 1976 · Vision Gallery, Boston, 1976 · Rochester Institute of Technology, 1977 · Everson Museum of Art, Syracuse, New York, 1977 · M.I.T. Creative Photography Gallery, Cambridge, 1978

Publications

35mm Photography

Selected collections

Museum of Modern Art, New York City; International Museum of Photography, George Eastman House, Rochester; Addison Gallery of American Art; New Orleans Museum of Art; Visual Studies Workshop; Sheldon Memorial Art Gallery, University of Nebraska, Lincoln.

Mr. Morse's original prints are color offset lithographs and appear on pp. 88 through 91.

JOHN RIZZO, *Lexington*

Born 1948, Boston
Education: University of Massachusetts, Amherst, B.A.; New England School of Photography.

John Rizzo is a free-lance photographer. He has taught photography at the New England School of Photography, Boston; the Boston Center for Adult Education; Middlesex Community College, Bedford, Massachusetts; Norfolk Correctional Institution, Norfolk, Massachusetts; and the Essex Photographic Workshop, Essex, Massachusetts.

Solo exhibitions

New England School of Photography, Gallery One, 1975, 1977 · Cary Memorial Library Gallery, Lexington, Massachusetts, 1978

Group exhibitions

Boston City Hall, Main Gallery, 1974 · Sherman Gallery, Boston University, 1975 · M.I.T. Creative Photography Gallery, Cambridge, 1978

Mr. Rizzo's black-and-white photographs appear on pp. 92 through 95.

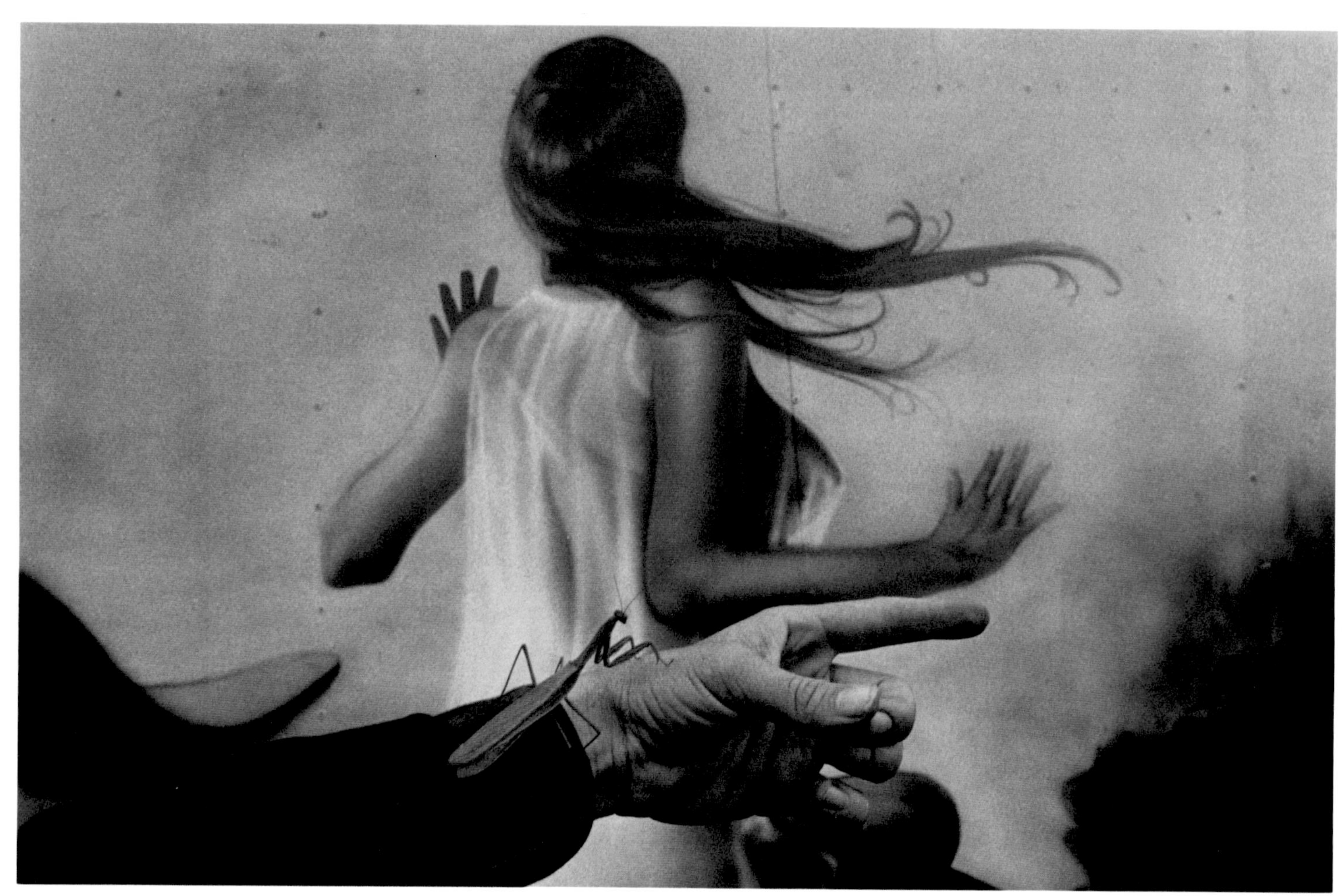

KEN BROWN · *1977*

68

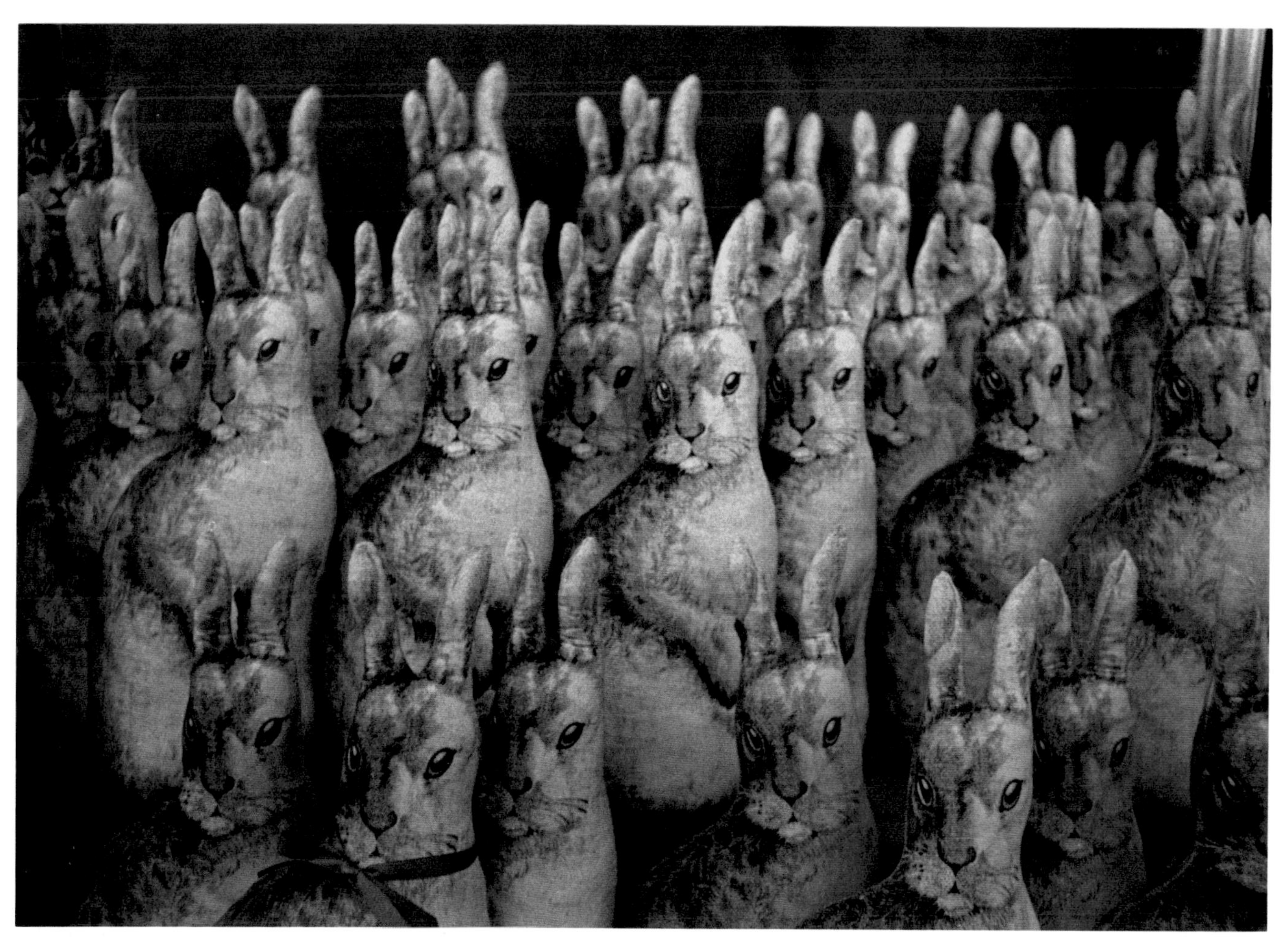

1975 · KEN BROWN

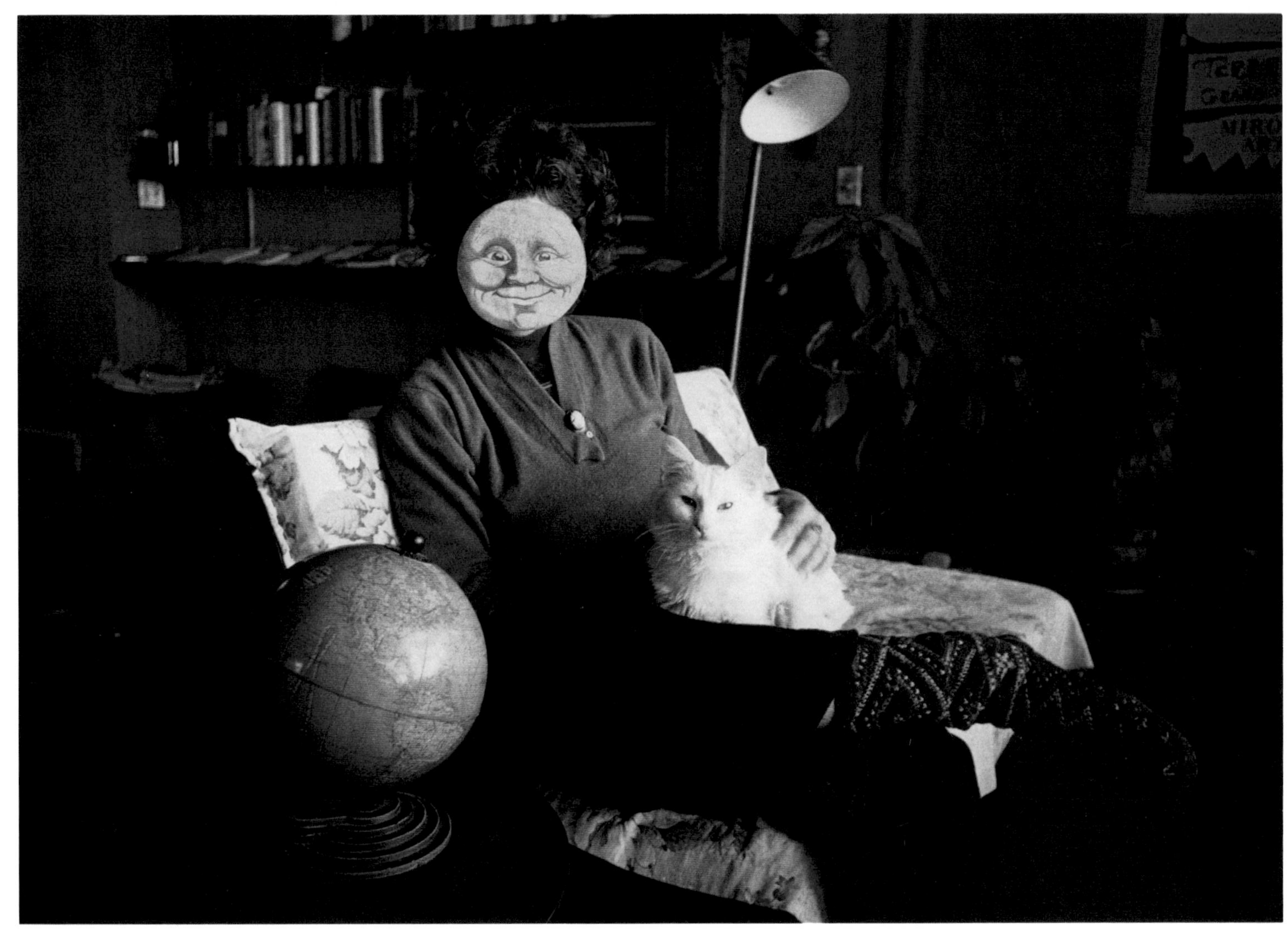

KEN BROWN · *1975*

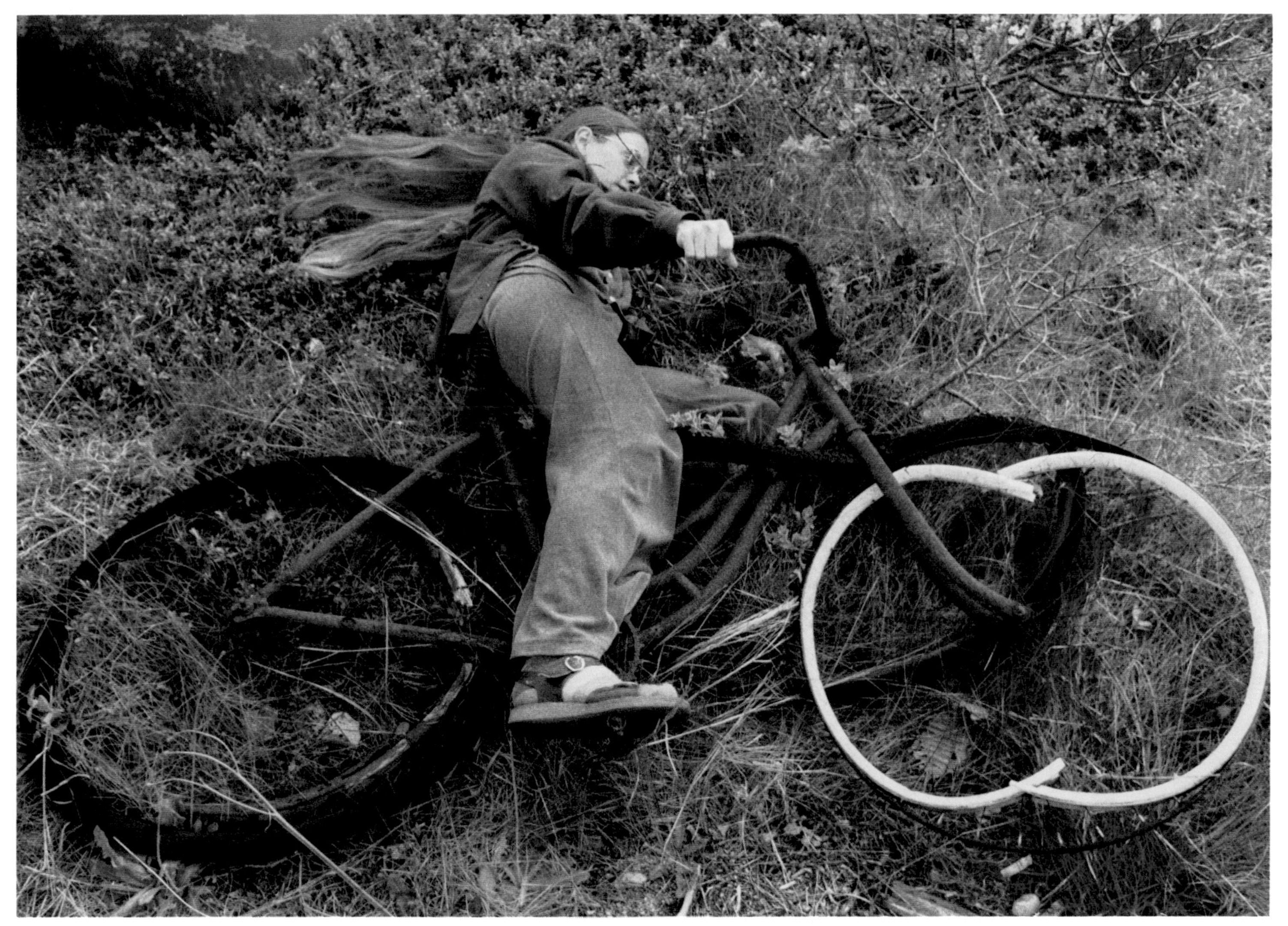

1975 · KEN BROWN

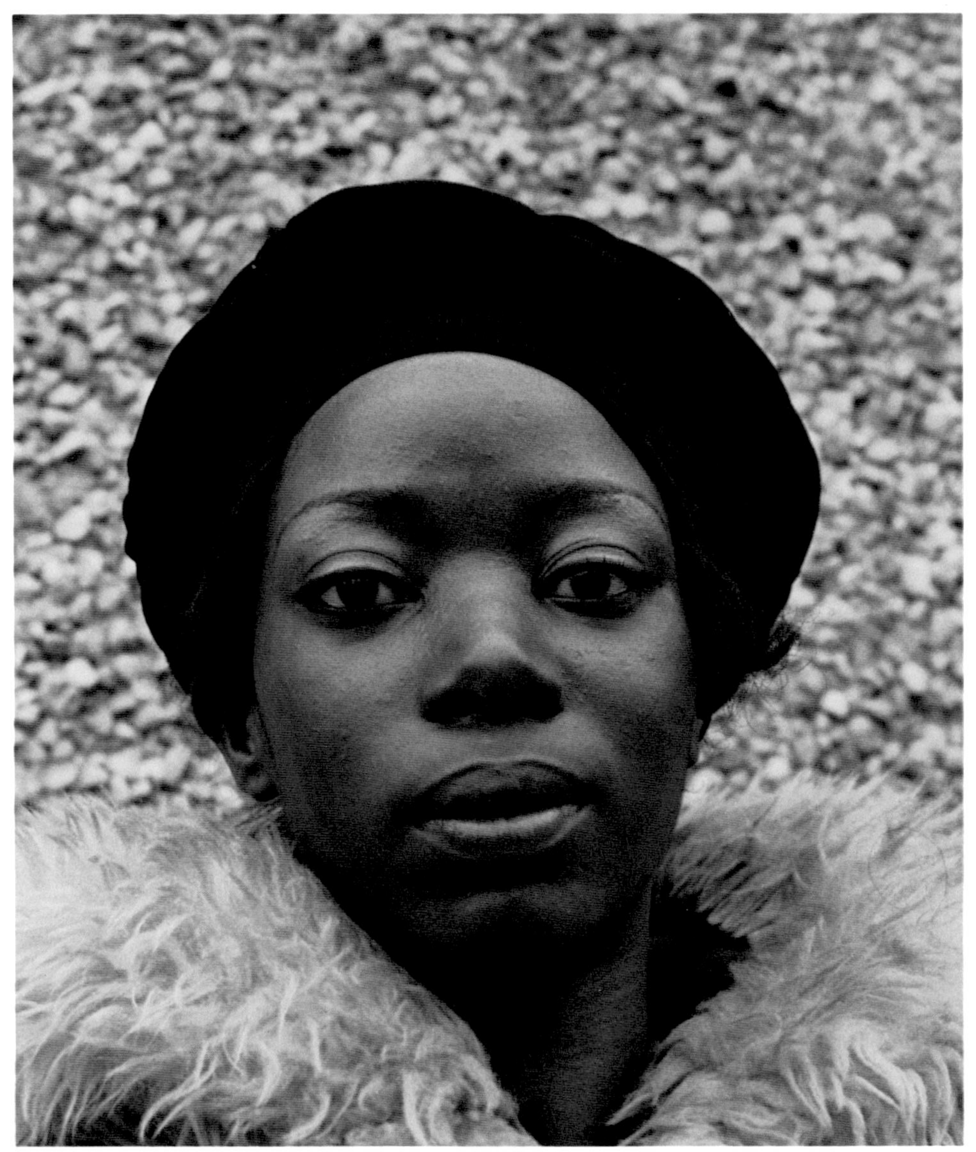

RUTH GREEN · *1976*

72

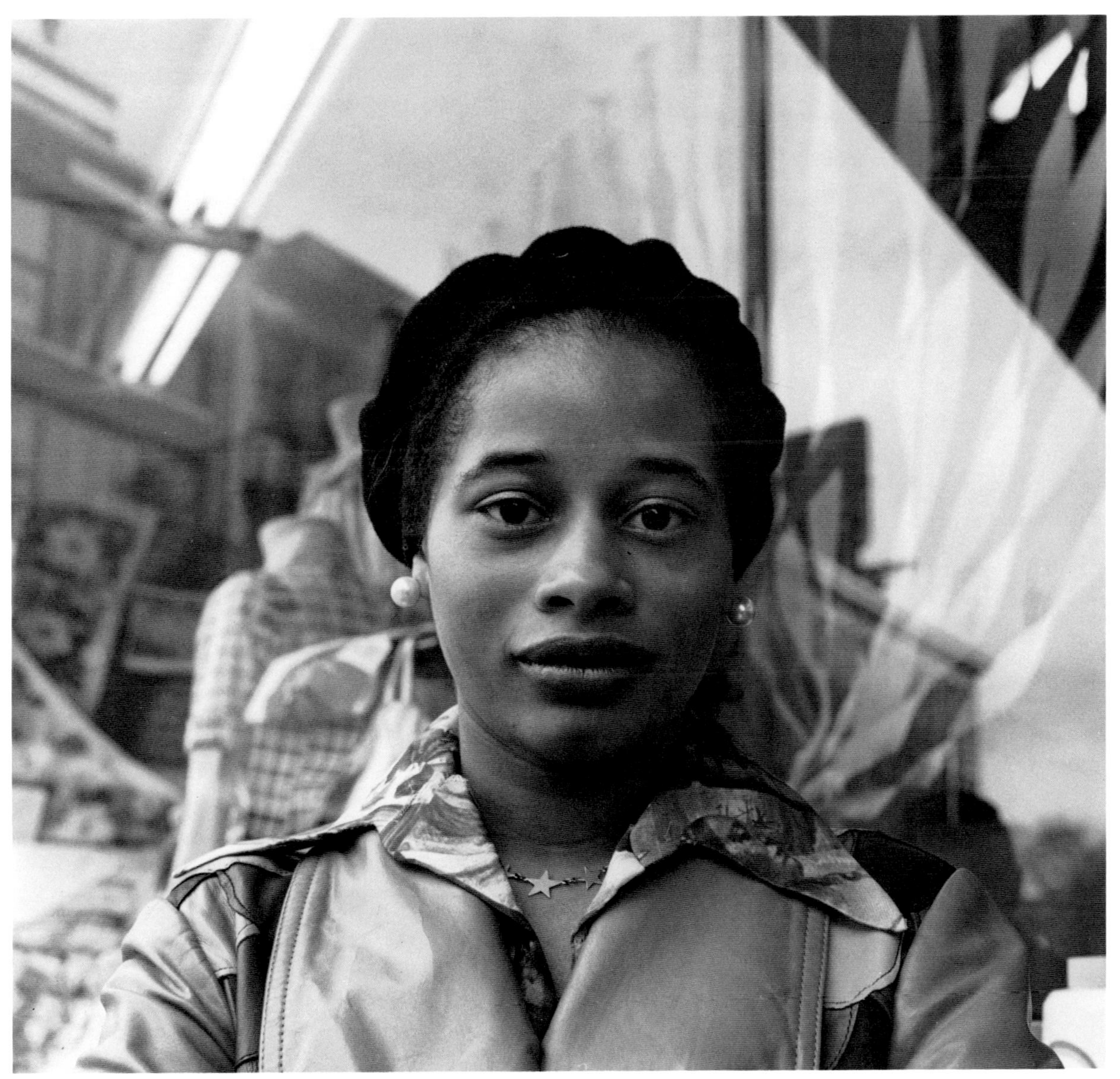

1976 · RUTH GREEN

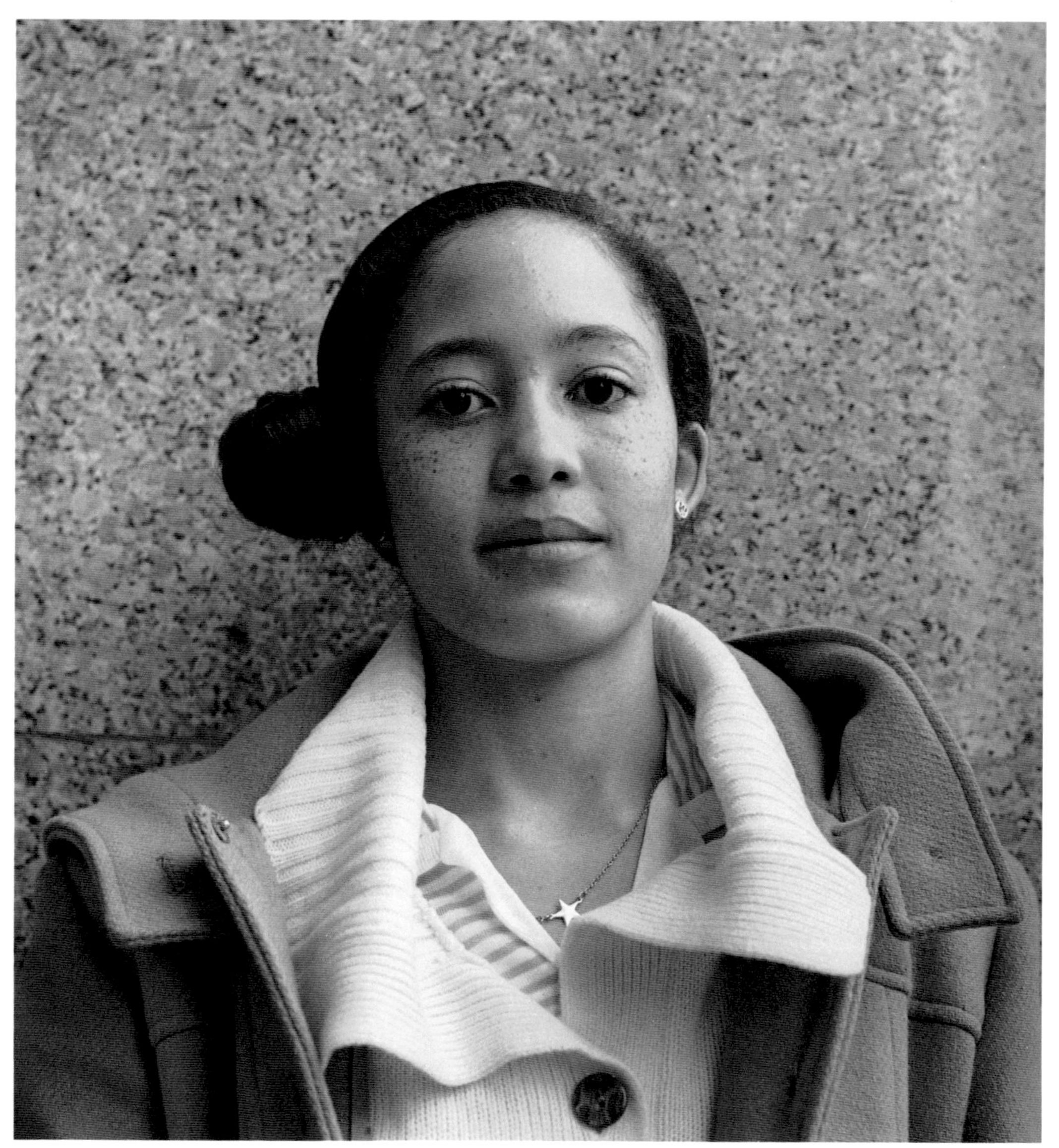

RUTH GREEN · *1976*

74

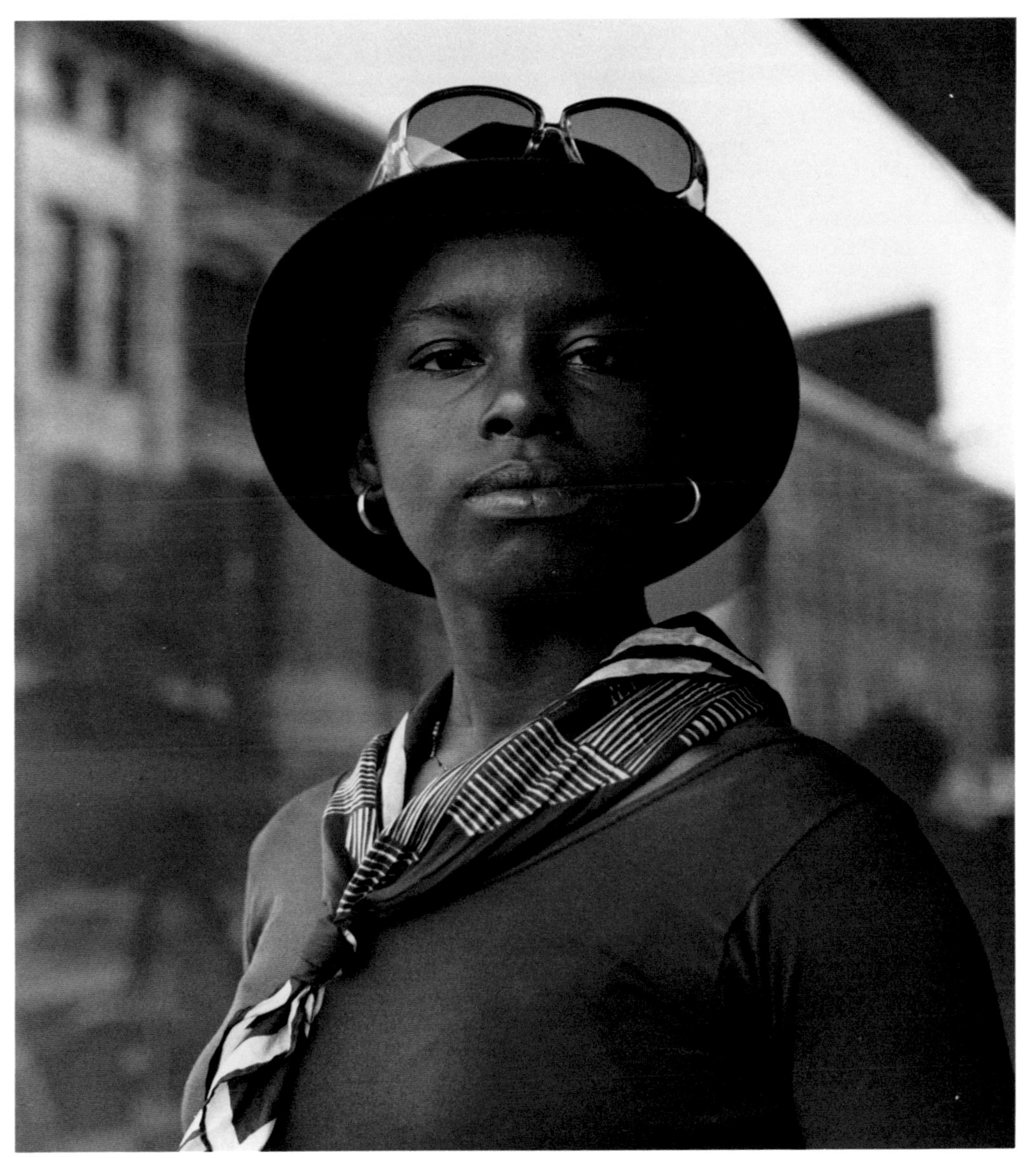

1976 · RUTH GREEN

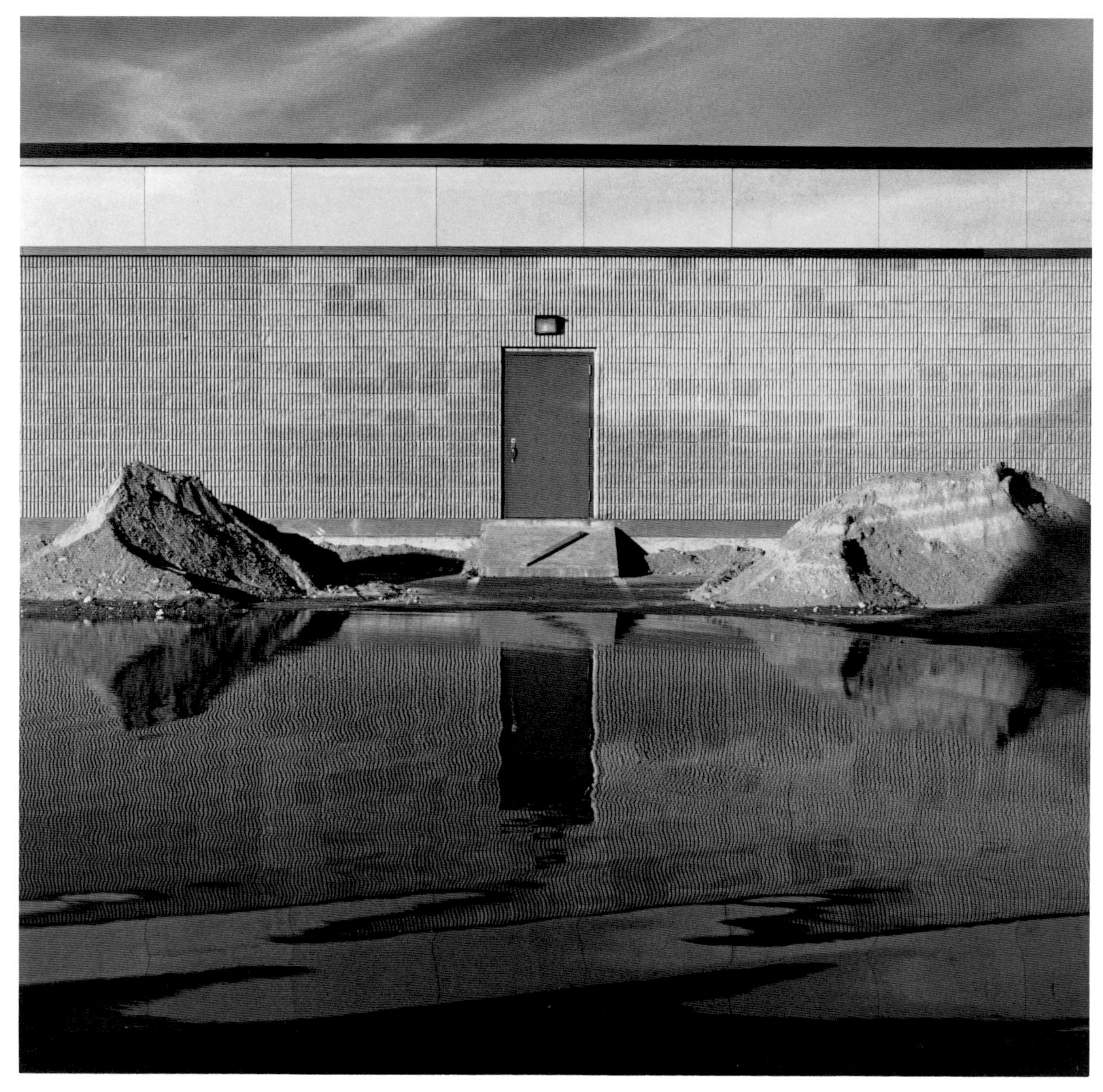

BRUCE KINCH · *Shopping Center, Burlington, Massachusetts, 1976*

76

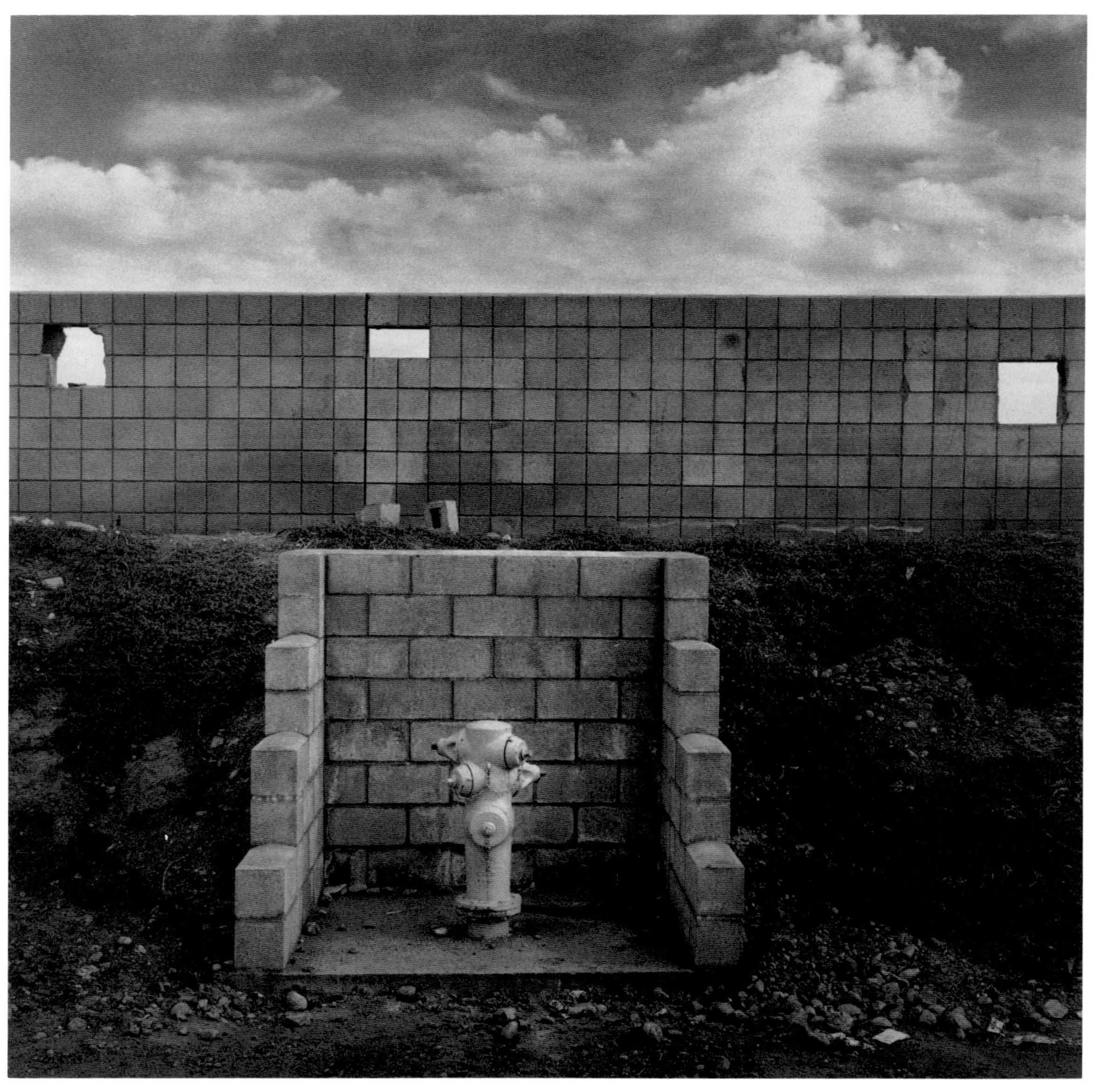

Mira Mesa, California, 1976 · BRUCE KINCH

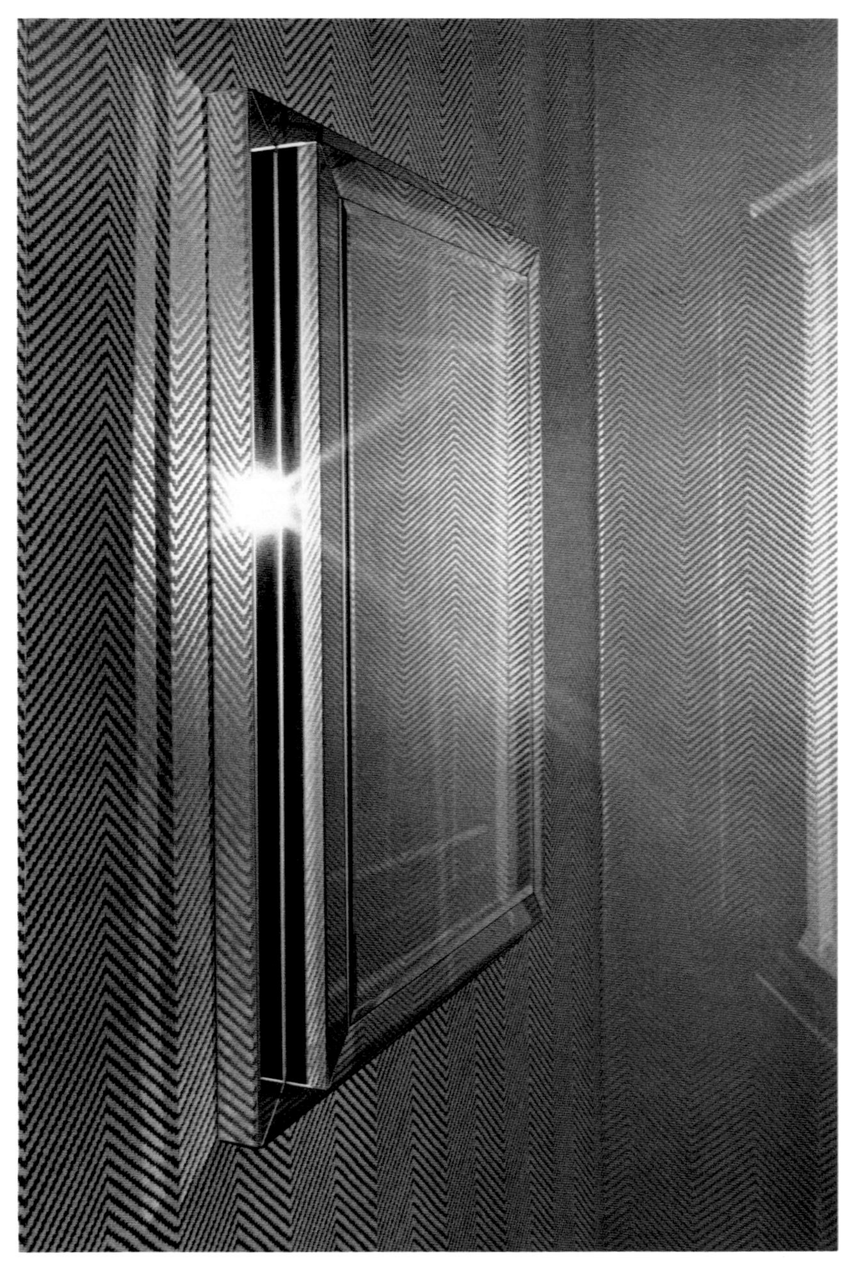

BRUCE KINCH · *New York, 1977*

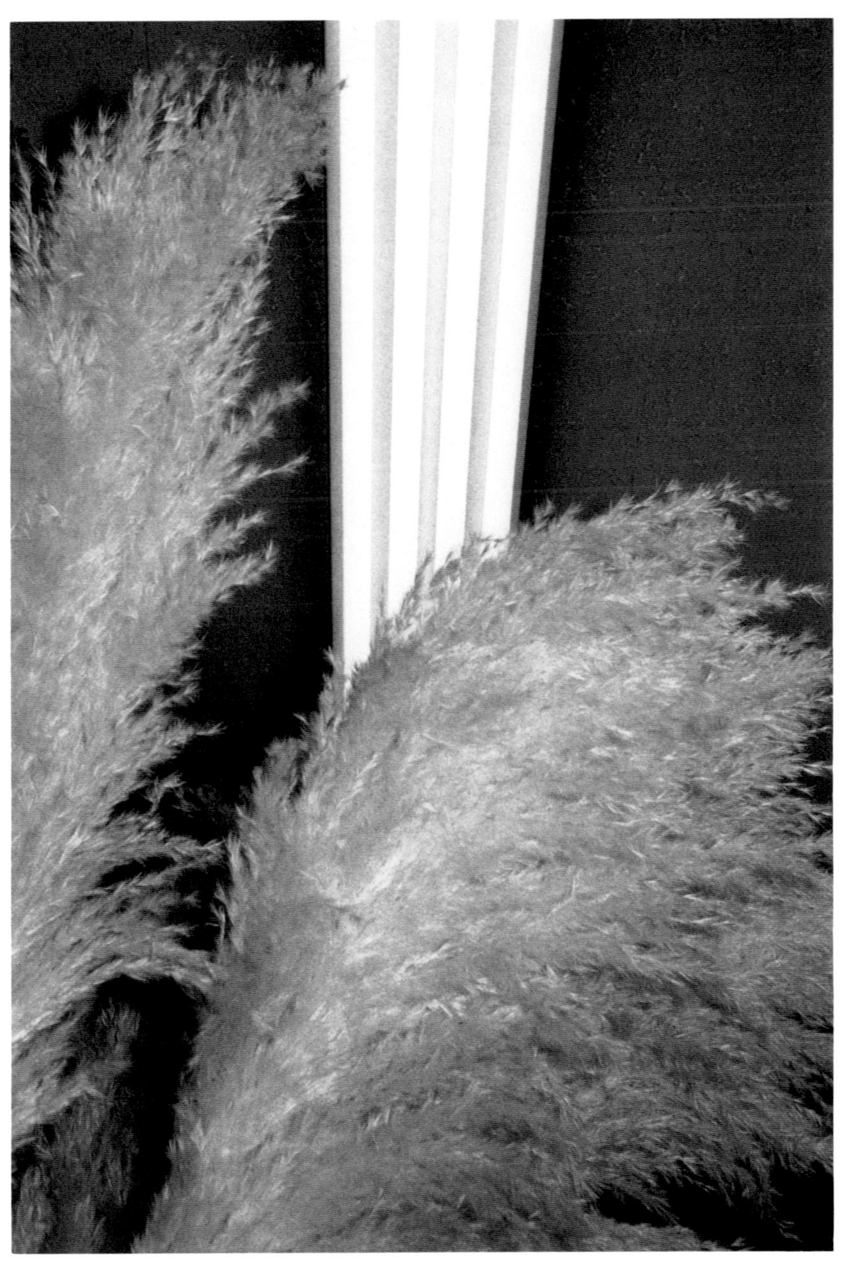

New York, 1977 · BRUCE KINCH

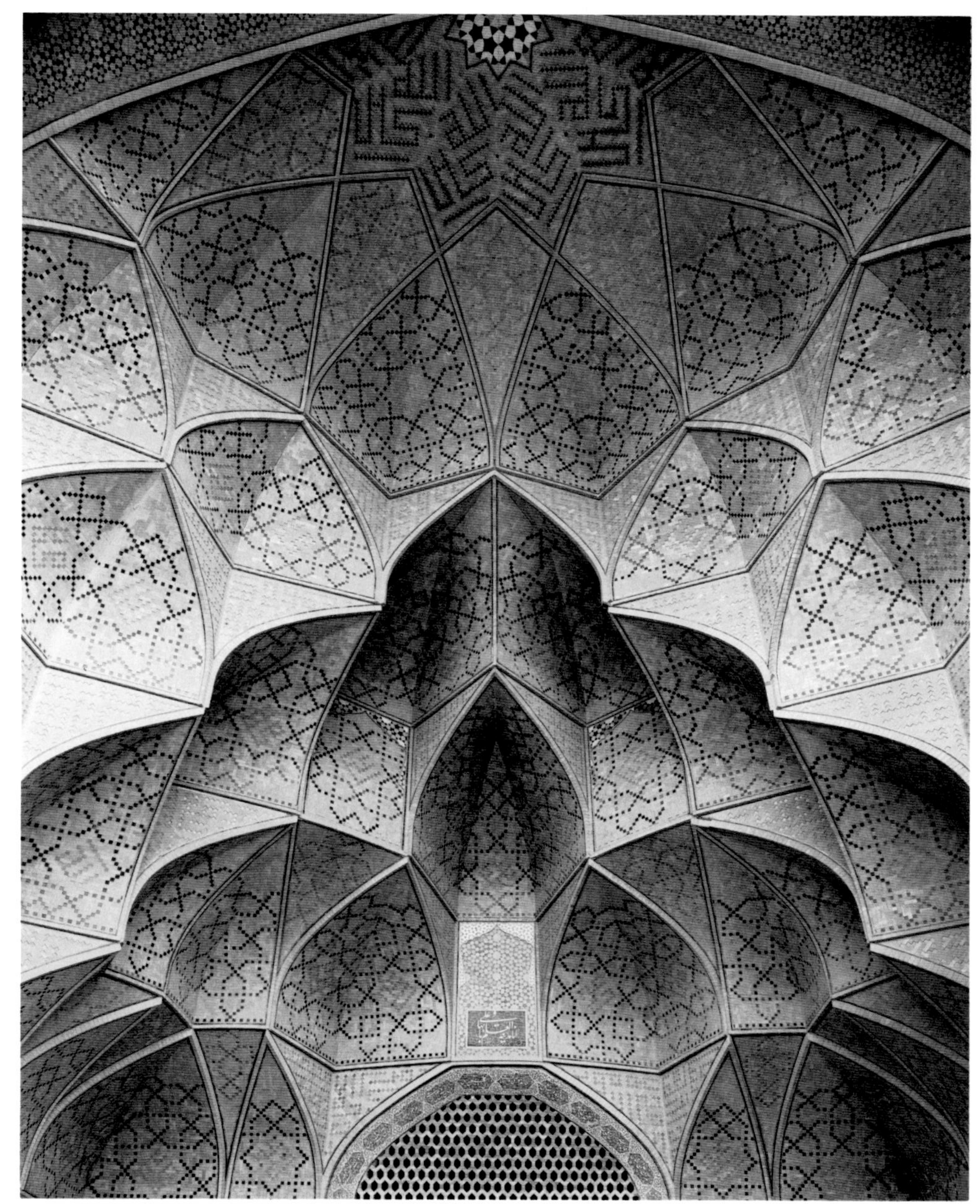

Isfahan #1, 1976

KIPTON KUMLER

80

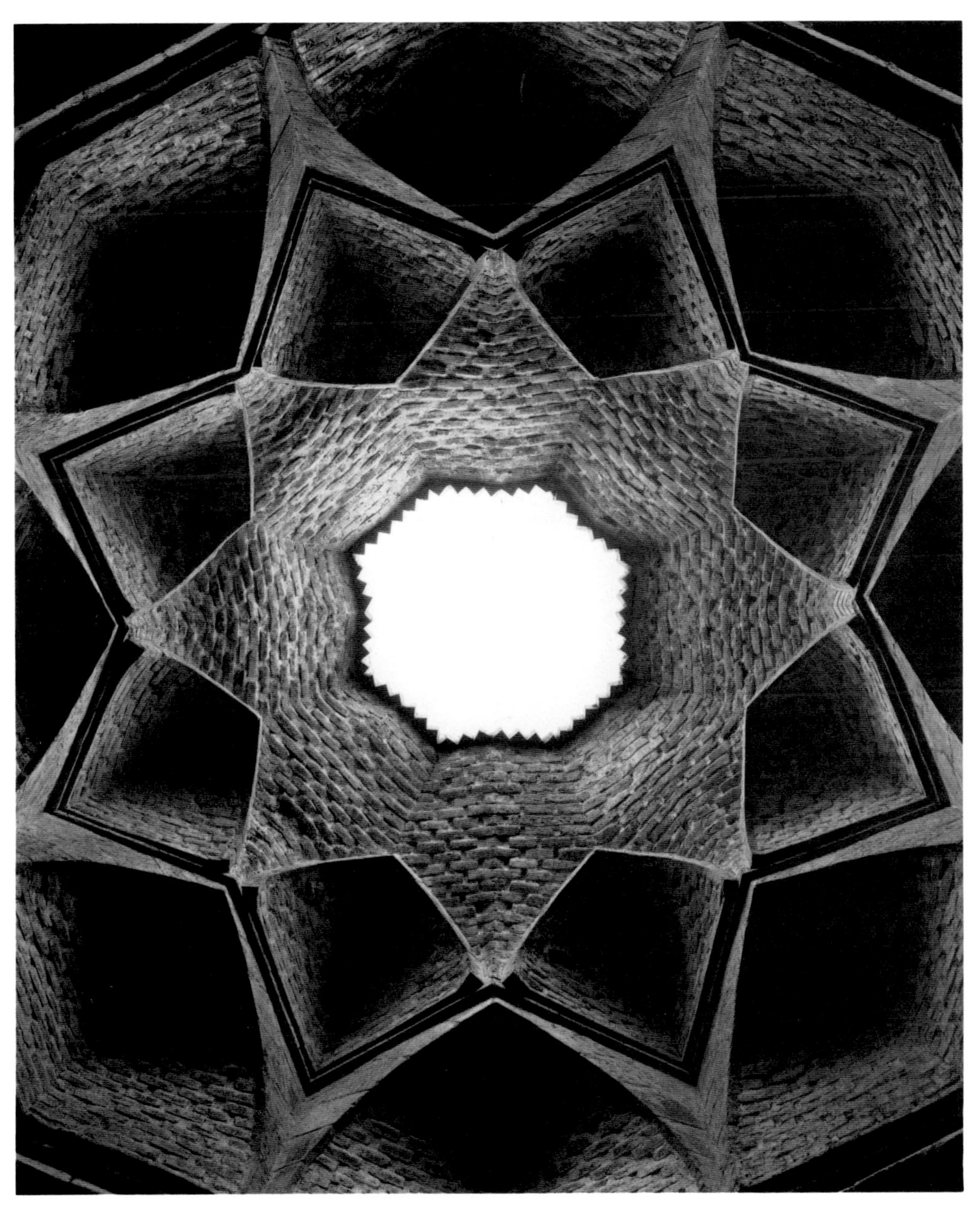

Isfahan #2, 1976

KIPTON KUMLER

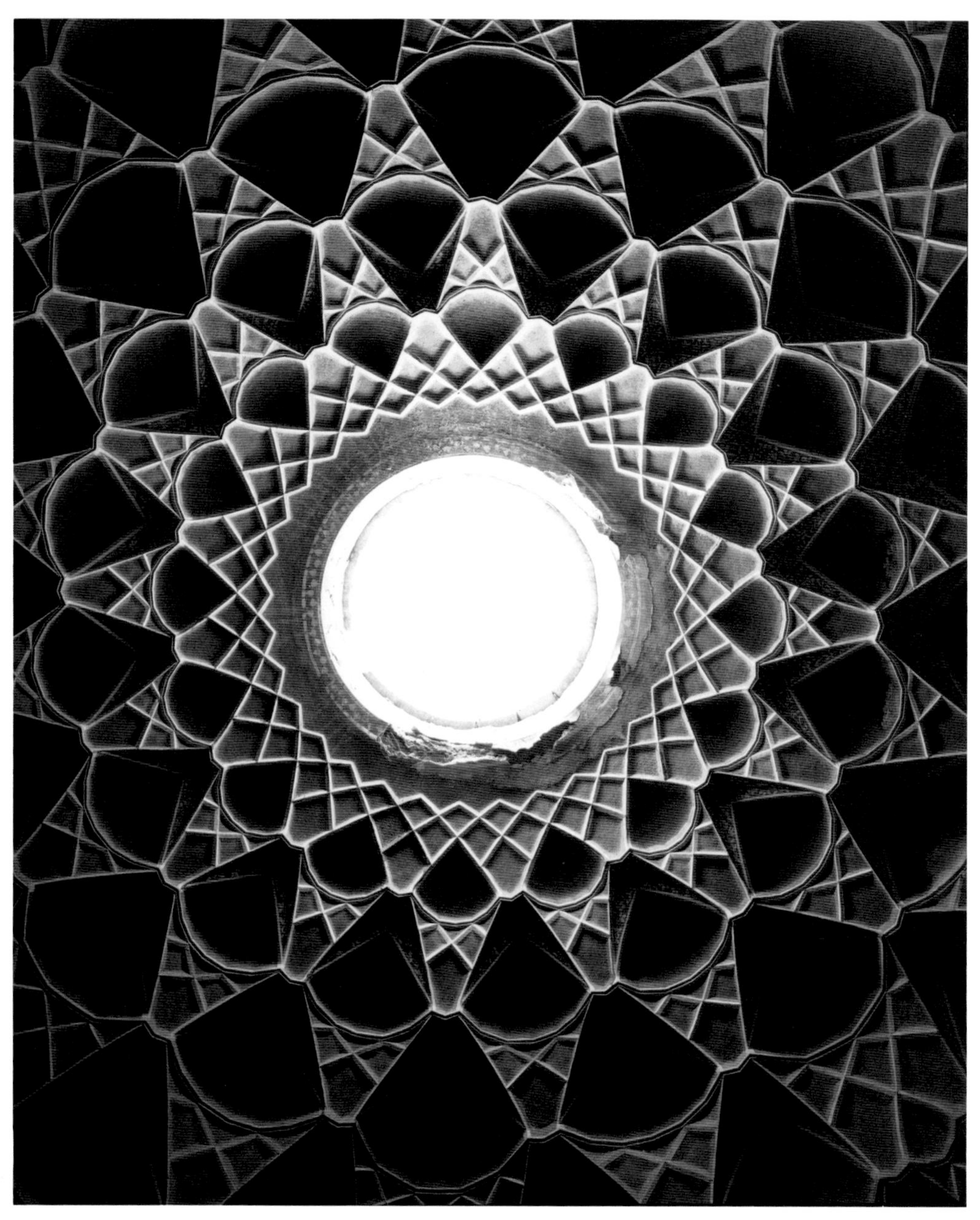

Keshan, 1976

KIPTON KUMLER

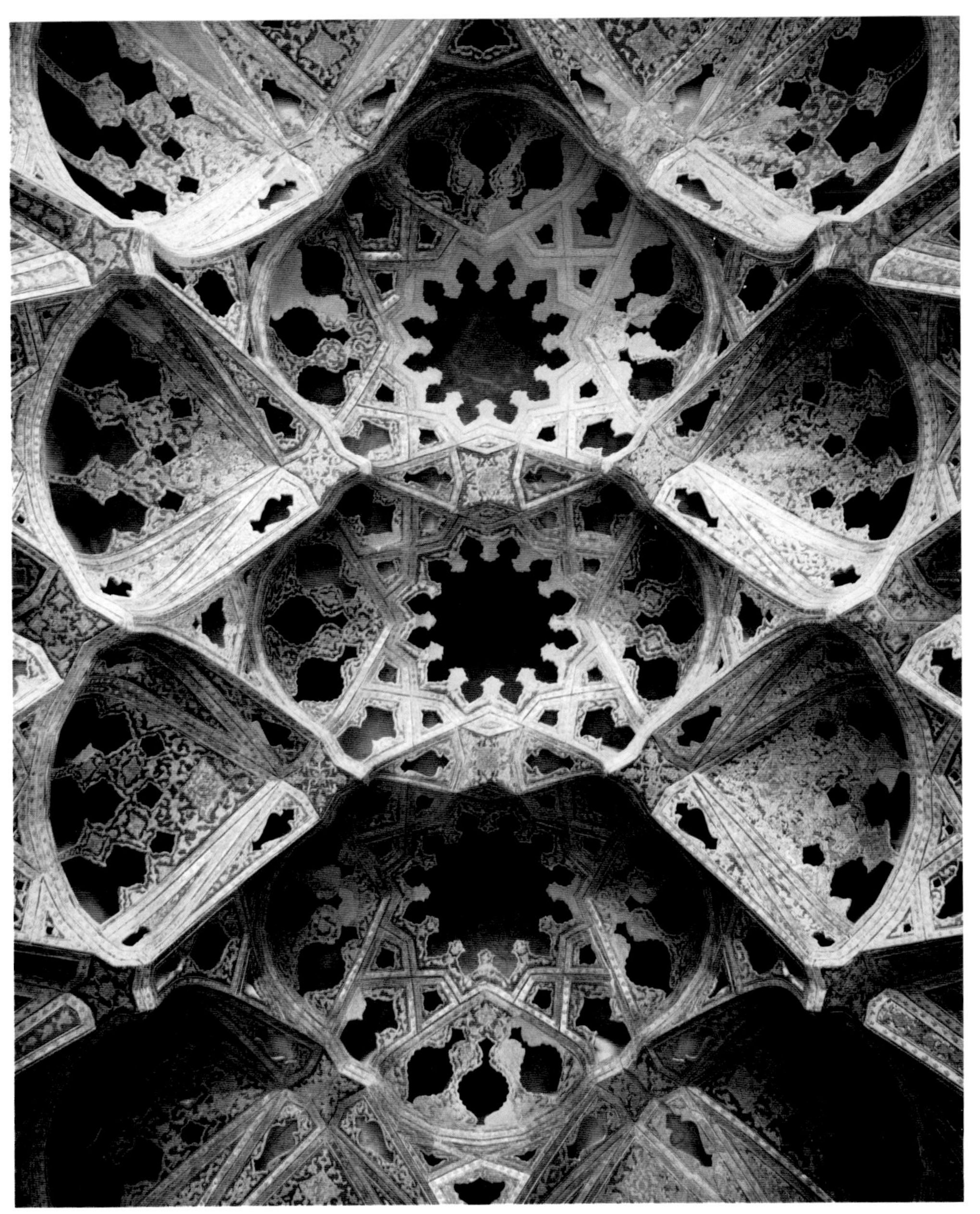

Isfahan #3, 1976

KIPTON KUMLER

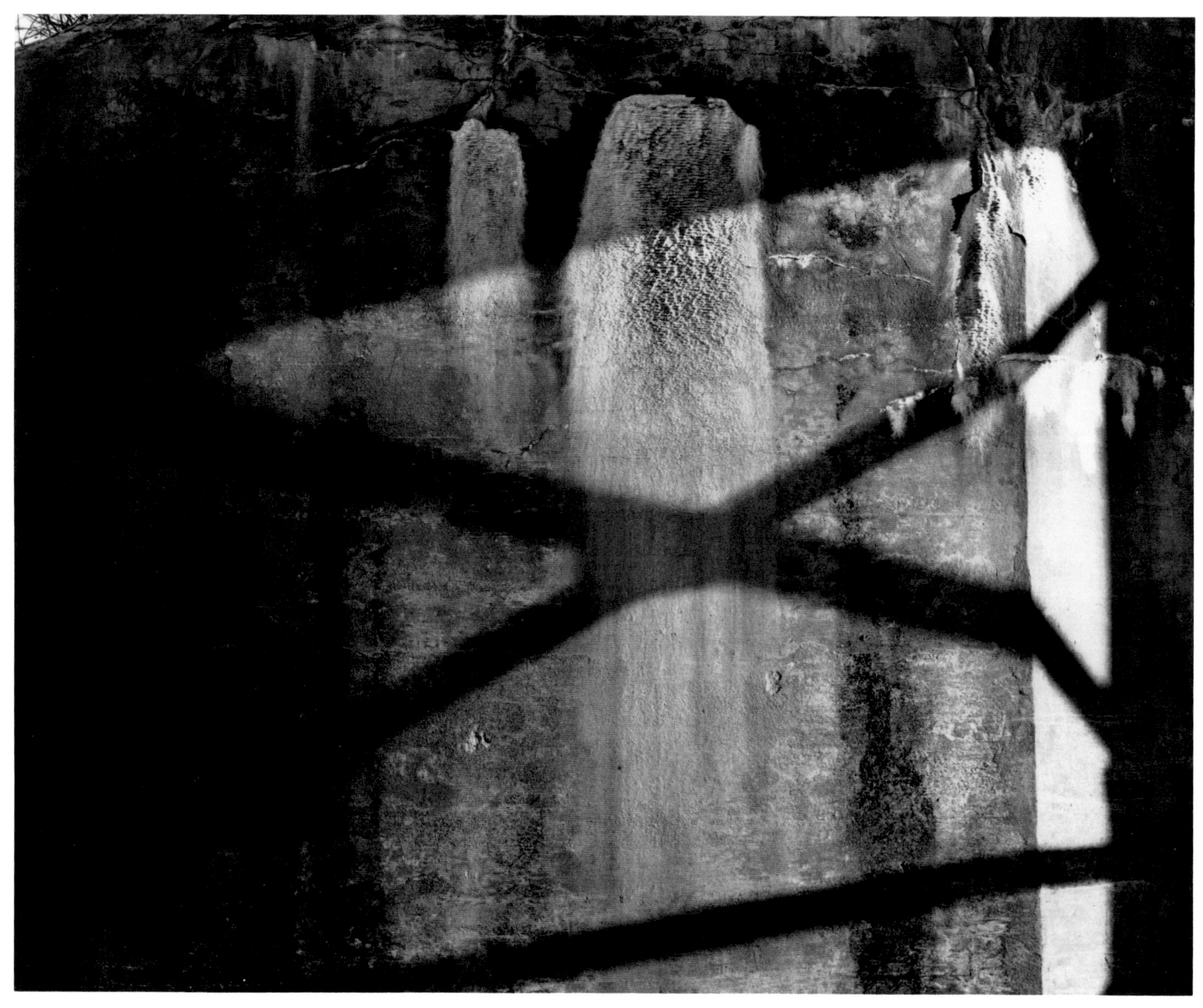

84

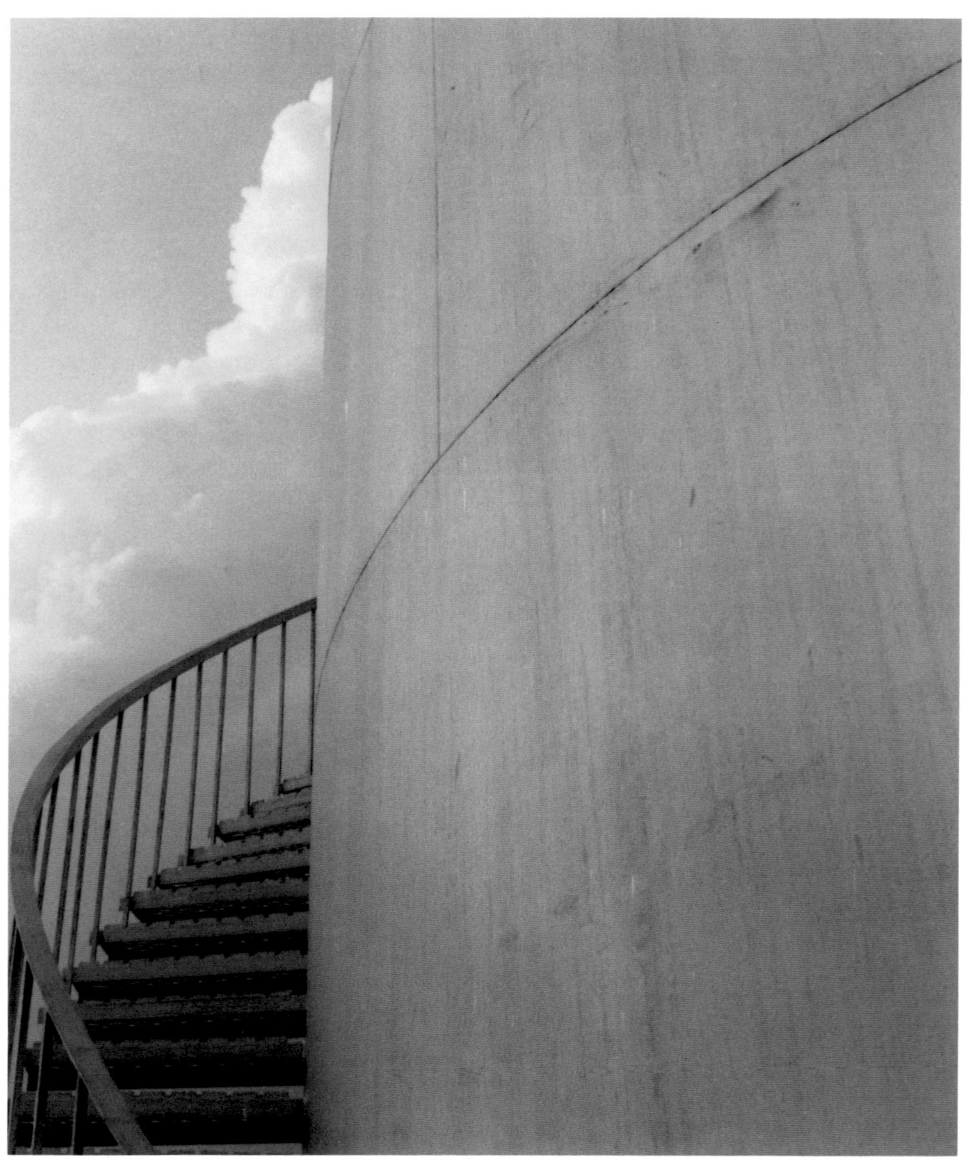

Keene, New Hampshire, 1975 · KEVIN MONAGHAN

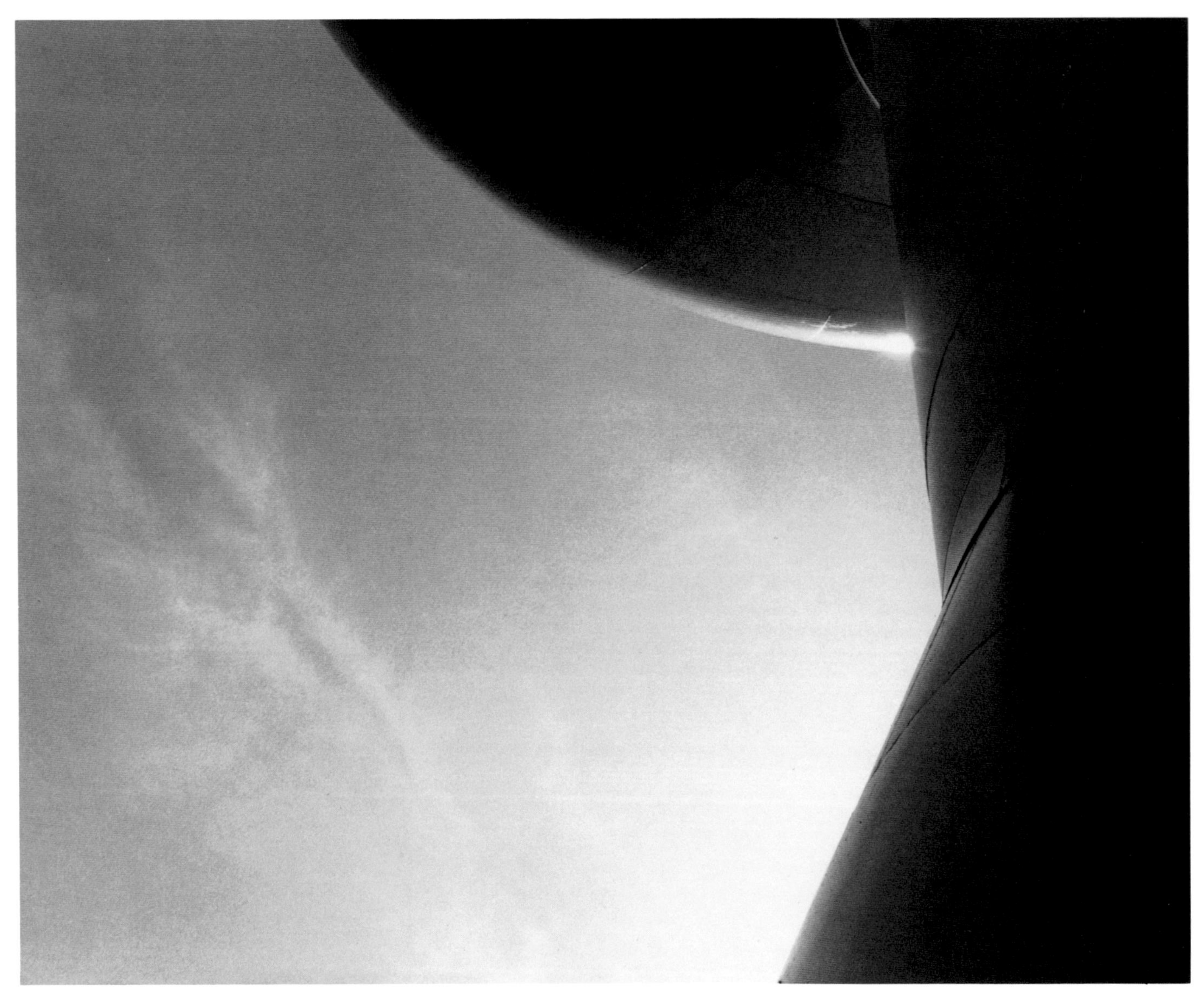

KEVIN MONAGHAN · *Madison, Wisconsin, 1976*

86

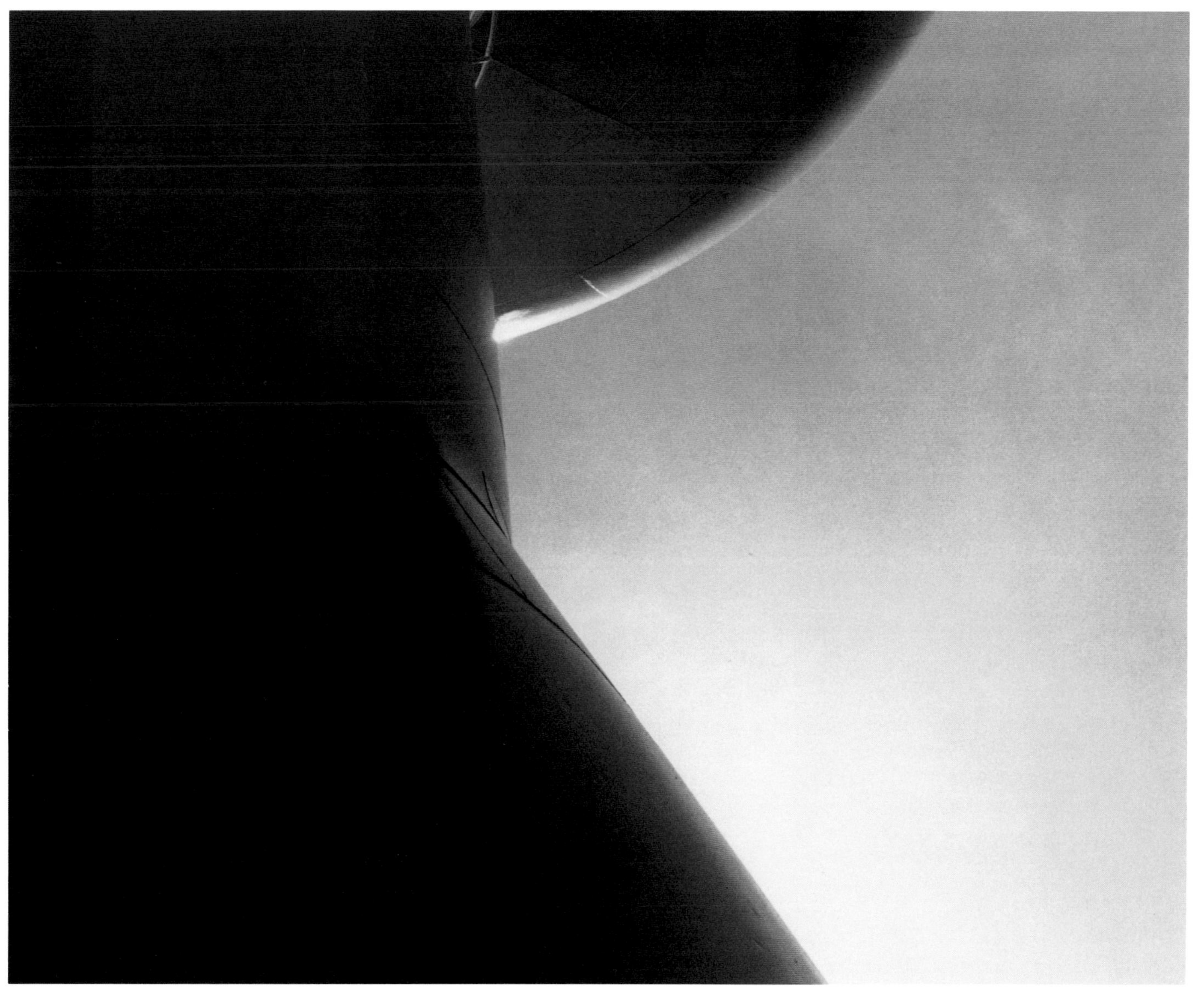

Madison, Wisconsin, 1976 · KEVIN MONAGHAN

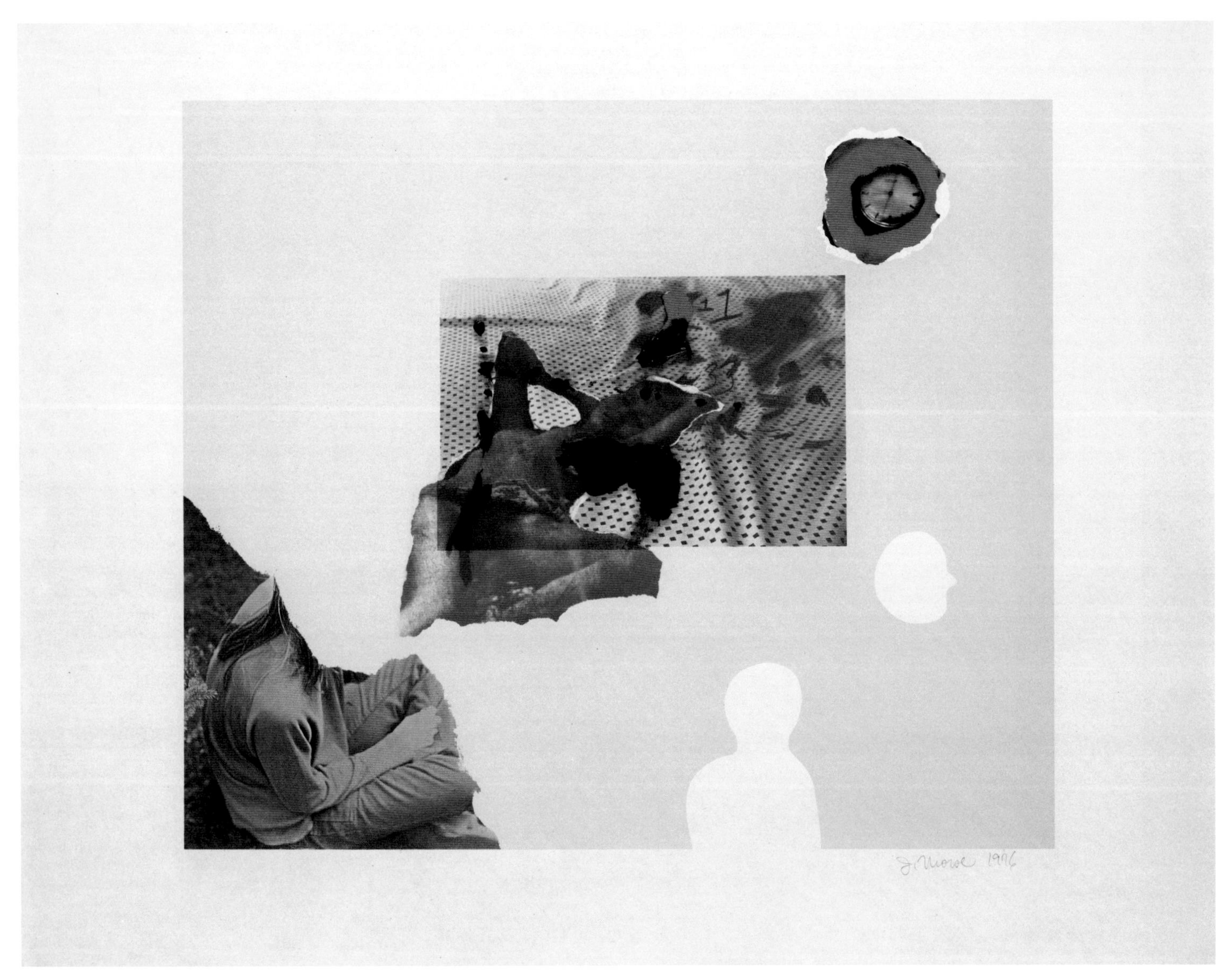

JONATHAN MORSE · *1976*

88

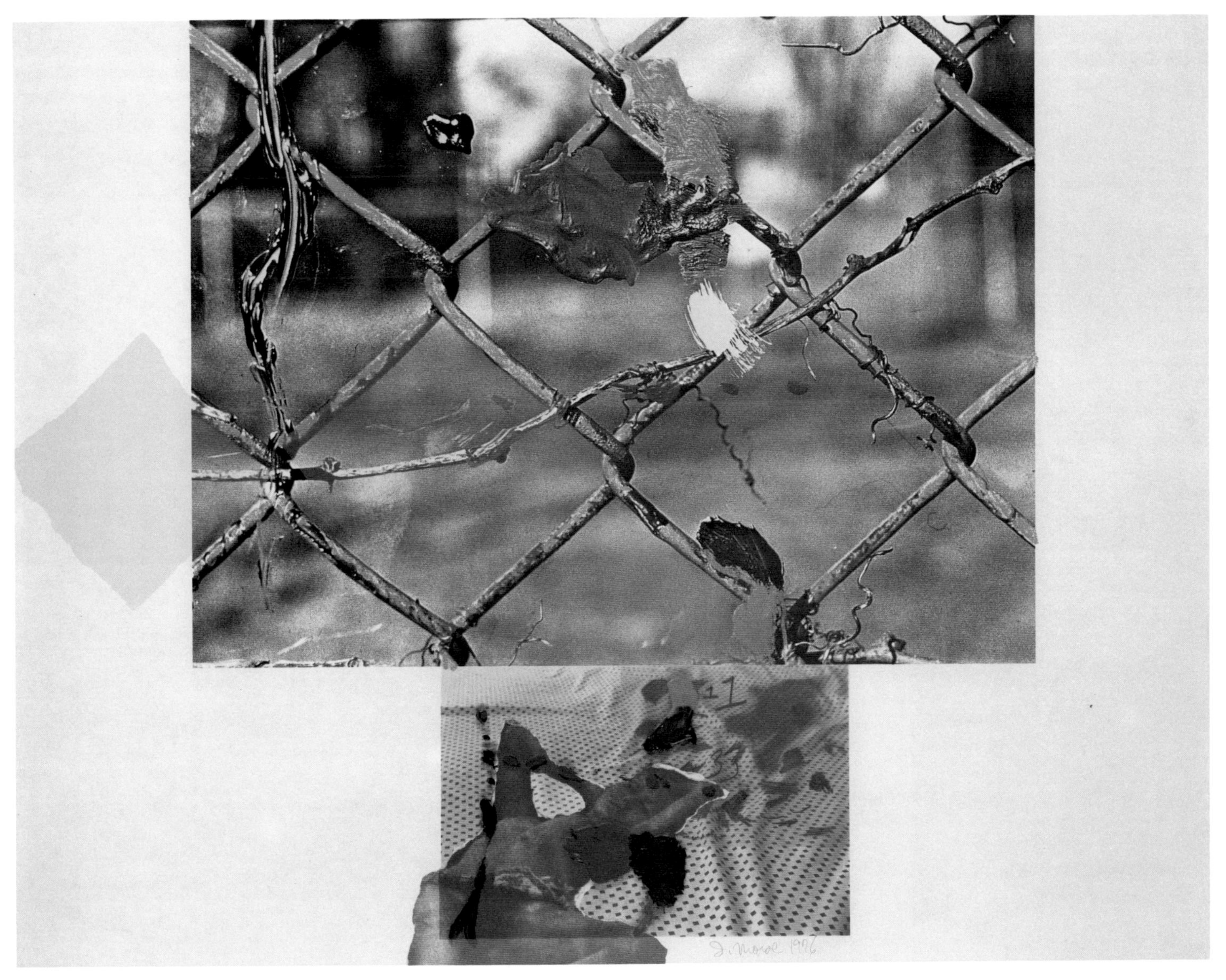

1976 · JONATHAN MORSE

JONATHAN MORSE · *1976*

90

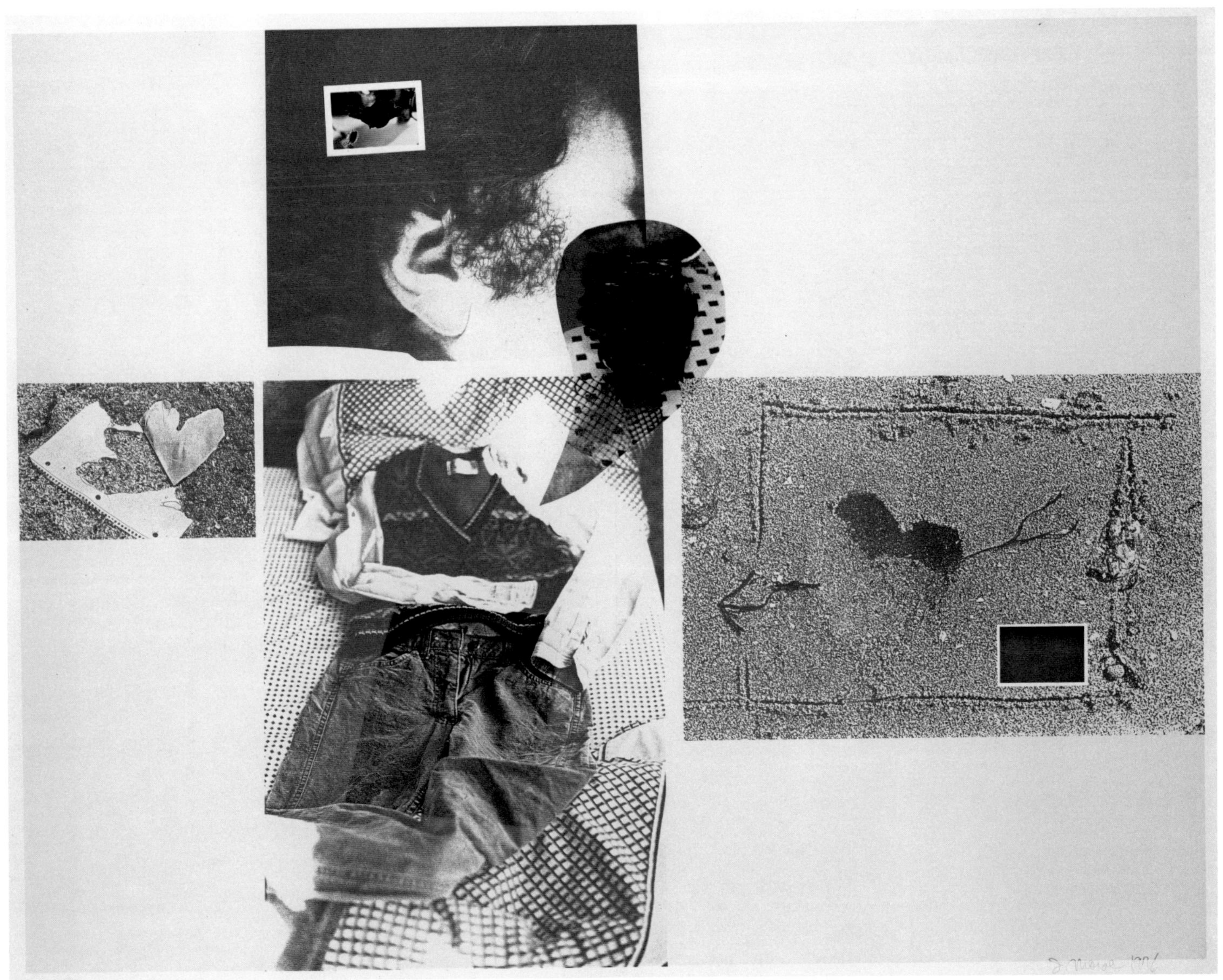

1976 · JONATHAN MORSE

91

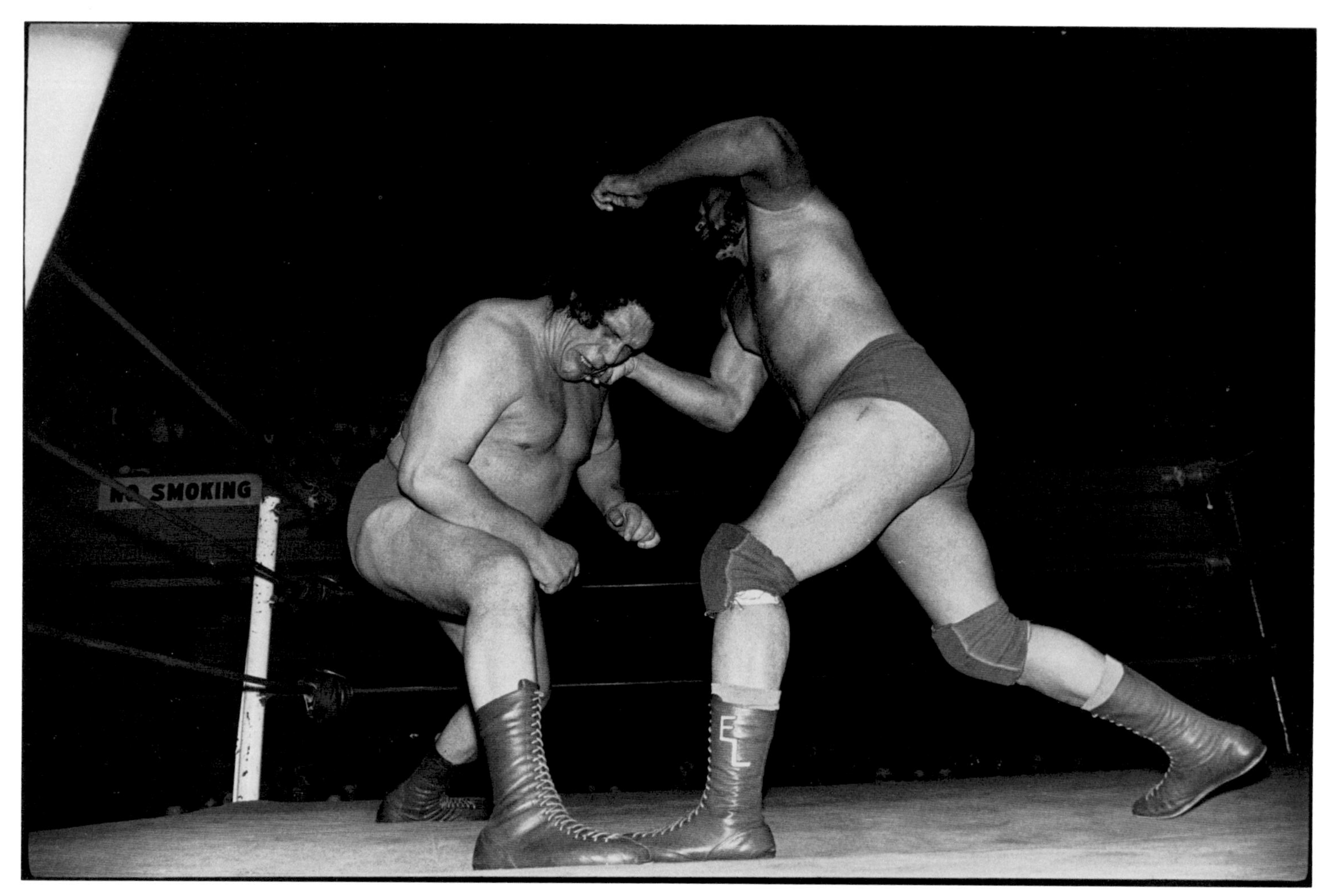

JOHN RIZZO · *Worcester, Massachusetts, 1975*

92

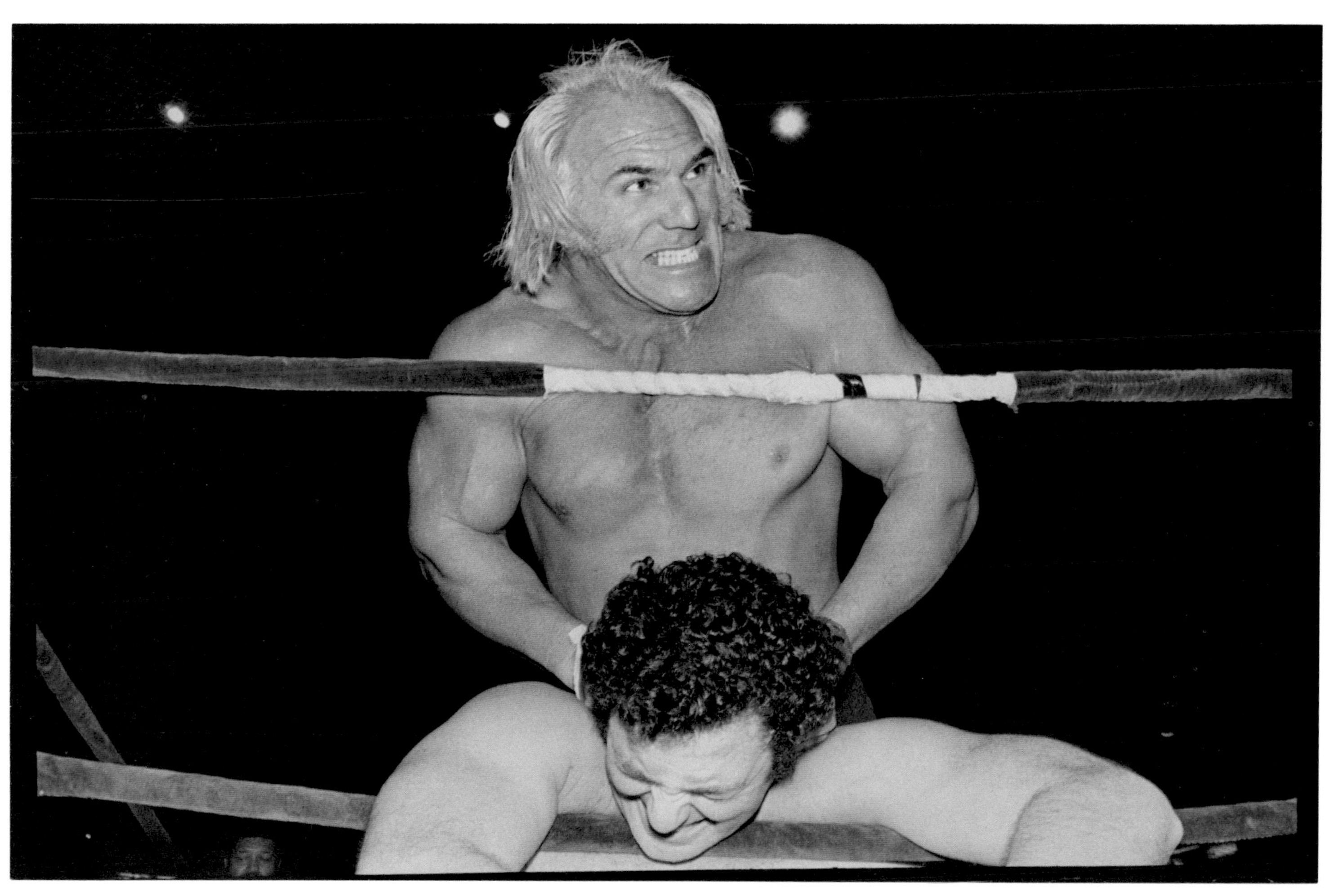

Boston Garden, Massachusetts, 1976 · JOHN RIZZO

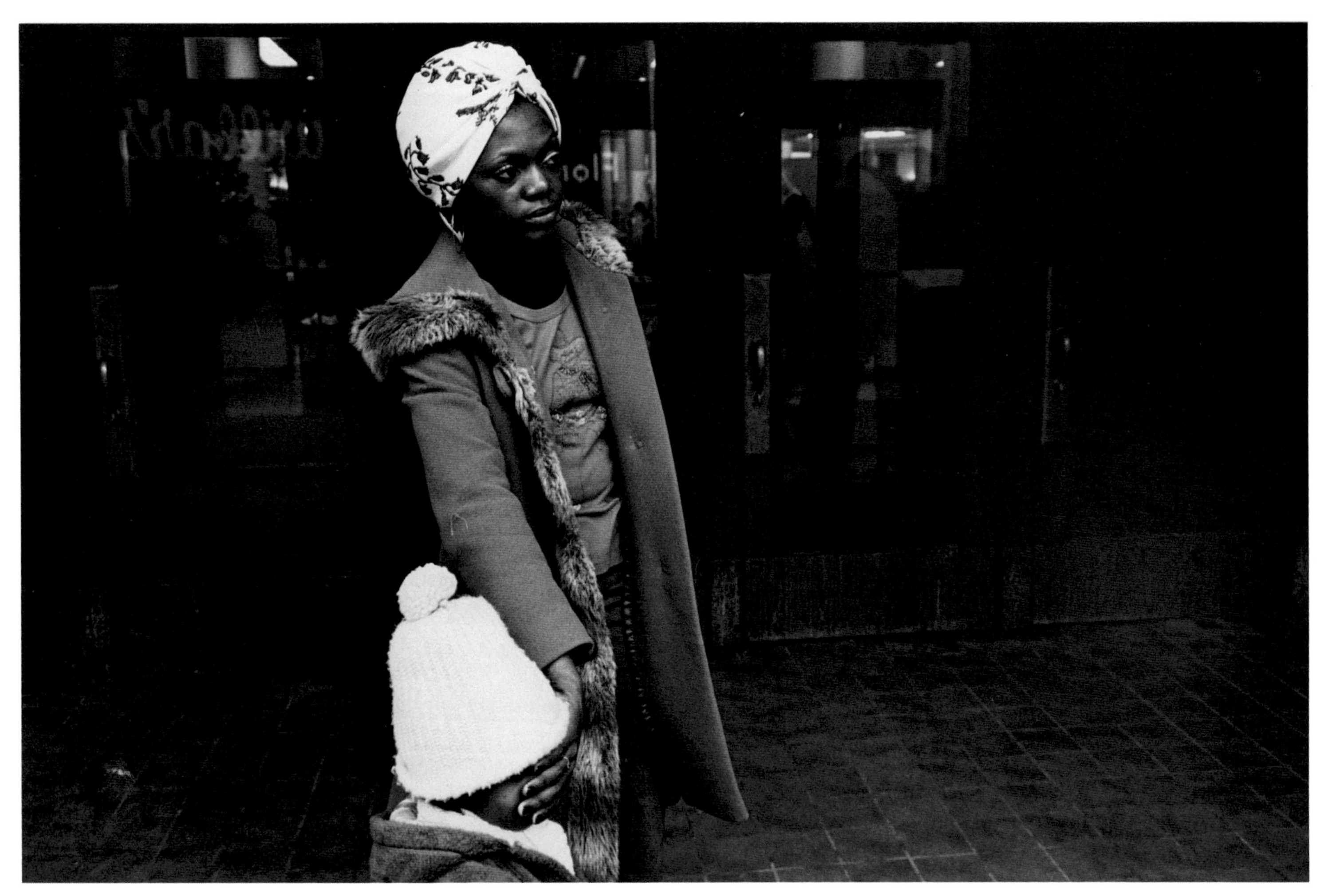

JOHN RIZZO · *Rochester, New York, 1973*

94

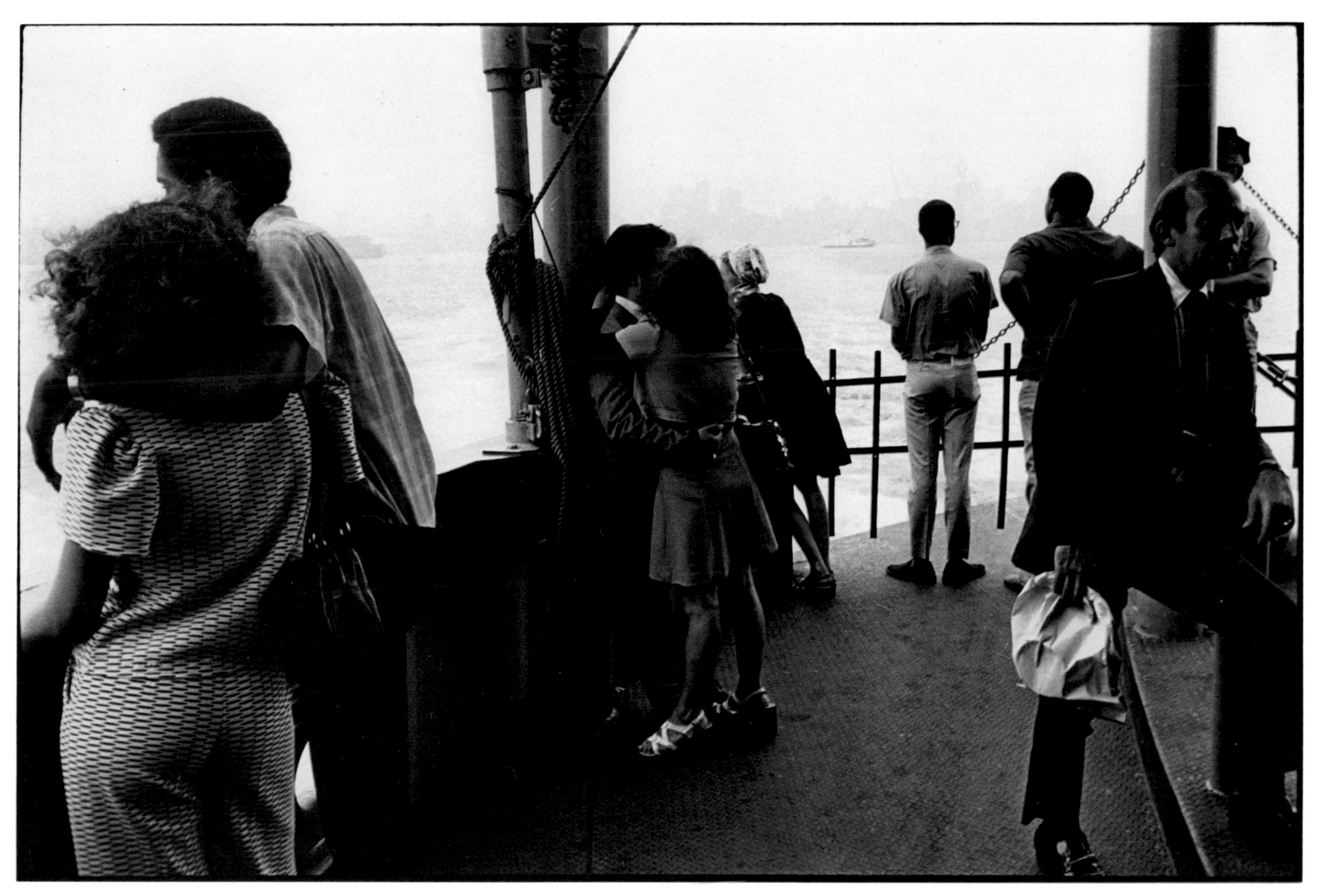

Staten Island Ferry, New York, 1975 · JOHN RIZZO

About the Foundation

In addition to the Artists Fellowship Program, the Massachusetts Arts and Humanities Foundation administers:

• the Artists in Residence Program, through which artists are paid to work as artists in schools and communities throughout Massachusetts;

• the Artists Living and Working Space Project, which is an effort to link artists' unique spatial needs with the needs of Massachusetts communities to recycle existing unused or underused commercial and industrial buildings;

• Lawyers for the Arts, an educational and legal referral service that conducts art law and art marketing workshops annually to bring together artists and legal and accounting professionals with specific interest and expertise in art law.

• The Research Program, a program that conducted (in 1977) the first empirical state-wide survey of visual artists in the United States. It continues to be a principal means of understanding the professional needs and objectives of individual creative artists in the Commonwealth.

For additional information about these and other services offered by the Foundation, write: Massachusetts Arts and Humanities Foundation, Inc., 100 Boylston Street, Boston, Massachusetts 02116. (617-482-8100).

The Foundation is a non-profit, tax-exempt organization. It is supported, in part, by the National Endowment for the Arts, a federal agency; the Massachusetts Council on the Arts and Humanities, a state agency; and a variety of other public and private agencies, private foundations, corporations, and individuals. Contributions to the Foundation are tax-deductible.